NATURE ON VIEW

Tokyo • SHUFUNOTOMO/WEATHERHILL • *New York*
PHOTOGRAPHS BY TOSHIAKI SAKUMA

NATURE ON VIEW

HOMES AND GARDENS INSPIRED BY JAPAN

Additional photo credits: Jack Donahoe 129-145;
Jean Mahoney 22, 27, 34-39, 50, 55, 58, 59, 69-71, 79,
88-91, 143, 145, 150, 152; Jon Jensen/Metropolitan Home
171, 172; Roland Reisley 9; Richard Robinson 174, 175;
Jeffrey Westman 108, 112-115; Ken Wyner 176, 178

Published jointly by Weatherhill, Inc.,
420 Madison Avenue, 15th Floor, New York, N.Y. 10017
and Shufunotomo Co., Ltd., 2-9, Kanda Surugadai, Chiyoda-ku,Tokyo, Japan

First Printing, 1993

Printed in Japan

ISBN 0-8348-0299-6
LCC Card No. 93-029192

Art Direction and Book Design
by Jean Mahoney

To J.R.D.
whose
insights
showed us
the way

C O N T E N T S

**The soft focus of rain on the garden...
an intimate courtyard rendered in snow...
a maple's brief burst of scarlet...
steadfast rocks changing in shifting planes of light.**

For centuries, peaceful images such as these have enlivened the traditional Japanese home. The vignettes are not framed works of art hung on a wall, but living dioramas created within small, private gardens. Designed to be viewed from the interior, they inseparably bind the house to the outside. The Japanese house cannot be considered without these displays. The garden extends the living space and offers a lifeline to mental and spiritual refreshment.

The integration of outside-inside space and its application to modern Western living is the theme of this book. As more and more Westerners gain exposure to life in Japan, many are borrowing essential principles of Japanese architecture for their own homes. Copying superficial embellishments of foreign architecture generally results in an unattractive hybrid; copying principles, however, retains the pleasing character of the original. Some of these ancient Japanese principles — a reverence for the landscape, the decorative use of structural elements, flexible space, a respect for natural materials, and the elimination of the extraneous — take on new meaning as developed countries emerge from an age of materialism to become more responsible custodians of the world's natural resources.

Japan's influence on modern Western home design is a long and well-documented history. We hope to add a new chapter to that story by providing a look at twenty-eight American homes which demonstrate the appeal and adaptability of timeless Japanese design to contemporary Western living styles and landscapes.

The people who created these homes are an essential part of our story. And they make us ask two questions: one, why did they gravitate towards an aesthetic distinctly different from their own? And two, how did they accomplish their goals? In a sense, each house was born in isolation. Although the homeowners were aware of the long evolution of Japanese-inspired houses in the U.S., they did not draw from it. They went to the primary source, Japan. Whether in actuality or in spirit, they relied on pure and traditional Japanese design as a starting template. In almost every case, the individuals involved were attracted to Japan's craftsmanship and its architectural tradition of inviting the outside in, or as Frank Lloyd Wright described it, the "blurred boundary" between inside and outside space.

This subtle merger has its antecedents in the idiogram that represents "home" in Japanese which is composed of two characters: *ka* for "house" and *tei* for "garden." It demonstrates the Japanese concept that only the addition of a garden makes a house a home. Unlike the Western world where the house and garden are separate entities, with the garden added after the house is built, if at all, the garden in Japan is an integral part of the design, and is not dependent on wealth or space. Even the humblest home in Japan finds a few square feet to turn into a symbolic reminder that man and nature are one.

Land poor, the Japanese treasure nature. Motifs from the natural world fill their art, and appreciation of the four seasons — and subseasons — informs their lifestyle. Their heightened awareness of nature, however, is not the result of its scarcity, but originates in their spiritual beliefs in Shintoism and Buddhism.

The ancient Shinto religion, which was largely animistic, believed that spirits resided in the rocks and trees and waterfalls. Trees in particular were revered since the tree was considered the means by which the gods descended to earth.

Buddhism, on the other hand, teaches that everything in the world, even the smallest stone, is governed by the same cosmic force. The Zen sect of Buddhism uses gardens for meditation, as places to acquire truth which is found not through scripture or teachings, but in sudden bursts of insight. This truth can be triggered by anything — a darting fish, the sound of the wind, even a group of stones. Nature's smallest components are believed to suggest the most profound thoughts.

Unfortunately, in contemporary Japan, the classic home with its contemplative garden is disappearing, crumbling under the bulldozers to make way for more high-rise buildings. Older residents who have spent their lives in these vintage dwellings report how insecure they feel in the new structures, deprived of the connection to nature. The sound of rain on the roof, the sight of the sheltering tree or the supple bamboo two steps away fill them with comfort. It is their *view* of nature, even without a conscious focus on the spiritual, that makes home a safe haven.

Traditional Japanese architecture has cast a long shadow around the world, far greater than its understated lines and humble manifestation in Japanese homes would suggest. And it is private residences that exemplify the heart of Japan's architectural tradition, not the temples, shrines nor public buildings.

The ability to view the outside from within stems from Japan's post and beam style of construction, which creates a large opening instead of a wall. Since the walls do not support the roof, they are hung like curtains on the structural framework. Whole sides of houses can be removed to open them up to the fresh air. The advent of the steel skeleton frame in the 1880's allowed the Western

The Walker House in Carmel, California, designed by Frank Lloyd Wright in 1948, unites with its rocky site and the lines of the sea.

world to develop this effect which has been known in Japan since at least the eighth century. Frank Lloyd Wright, who practiced "organic architecture," as well as the architects of the Bauhaus School — Mies van der Rohe, Walter Gropius and Le Corbusier — derived key concepts from Japan and began creating open, flexible space tied to the outdoors. Gropius and Wright also used a standardized shape as a design unit and favored built-in storage and low level furniture, all Asian concepts. Although Western architects in turn taught Japan how to build with brick, iron and steel, transforming the skyline of its modern cities, the ancient principles that guided its master carpenter/architects are also still being used in Japan with renewed enthusiasm as the 20th century comes to a close.

Foremost among these architects was Wright, indisputably America's greatest architect, who said in 1914 that his designs "owed a debt to Japanese ideals." One of the most important interpreters of traditional Japanese architecture, he confided in *An Autobiography,* "Japan has appealed to me as the most romantic, artistic, nature-inspired country on earth...The Japanese house naturally fascinated me and I would spend hours taking it all to pieces and putting it together again...At last I found one country on earth where simplicity, as natural, is supreme." Wright was the master of a form called the Prairie house, an outgrowth of his Mid-Western landscape. "The prairie has a beauty of its own," he wrote, "and we should recognize and accentuate this natural beauty, its quiet level." To do this, he used low proportions, sheltering overhangs, low terraces and out-reaching walls sequestering private gardens, all hallmarks of the Japanese house.

Wanting to accentuate the beauty of their various locales, the creators of the homes in this book

Wright adapted Japan's hovering roof and curtain walls for the five-bedroom home designed in 1951 for Roland and Ronny Reisley in New York.

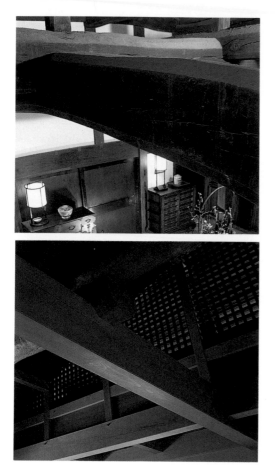

began with only mental pictures of what they hoped to attain. Finding the professionals needed to achieve their expectations was time-consuming and often frustrating. One of the homeowners involved, Helga Fleishman, who is an expert on Japanese art, expressed the gap between ideal and execution this way: "Studying the Japanese aesthetic is similar to learning a foreign language. One understands language before one can speak correctly. Similarly, I can recognize great Japanese screens, lacquer and porcelain design. Yet I cannot even arrange flowers to please a Japanese eye." The help she and her husband, Phillip, found to recreate the Japanese aesthetic — and the success of others with parallel quests — is documented in this book with the hope that readers will find it both useful and encouraging.

Precise, geometric and uncluttered, Japanese aesthetics rest in construction techniques. As Len Brackett, a specialist in the building of Japanese houses in the U.S., explains, "Very little is done for effect alone, so the result is a simple, elegant and honest structure with few embellishments to detract from its lines. All Japanese architectural forms are dictated by the system in which two pieces of wood are joined together in the nicest, strongest, most permanent way."

Post and beam construction begins with a structural cage whose components are pre-cut to interlock without nails. The joints are prepared in advance and the framework is erected at the site all at once. This technique is not unlike the timber frame construction that characterized building in the U.S. until the 20th century and which is now undergoing a renaissance at the start of the 21st century. However, the Japanese are the unrivaled masters of joinery; their sophisticated and beautiful joints are admired by carpenters everywhere. Because the best woods are used, joints never open. Some woods are air dried for years to insure stability. Sliding wall panels, for example, continue to glide effortlessly in their tracks, without metal assists, after years of use despite wide changes in temperature and humidity. The interlocking joints make the entire house highly flexible, allowing it to twist and give — and not collapse — during earthquakes. The rap of a mallet can realign components afterwards. Traditional Japanese construction bears a certain resemblance to Tudor architecture where the structural cage is also left exposed. However, Tudor architecture is braced with diagonal supports and is expected to remain rigid.

The Japanese house is essentially one room, which is configured into smaller compartments by movable walls that can be slid one behind the other or removed completely. One area can serve many functions in sequence: eating, entertaining, working, sleeping. Or, all interior walls can be removed to accommodate a large gathering. Partly from lack of space — 80 percent of Japan's population lives on ten percent of the land — and partly from a belief that small space conveys *wabi* or "calm simplicity," rooms are kept to a minimal size. Even exterior walls, usually wooden grids called *shoji* which are paned with light-diffusing paper, can be removed to open the house to the outdoors. In summer, the solid winter walls mounted on outer tracks to protect the *shoji* can be replaced by reed and bamboo sliding panels to allow breezes to penetrate the interior.

Although man has for centuries built with stone, traditional Japanese architecture favors wood in its natural state. Historically, wood, paper, straw and mud were all readily available so that the indigenous architecture prospered with everyday materials. Wood used in construction is rarely painted or made to look like another material to retain the resemblance to nature's beauty.

Another fundamental feature of Japanese architecture is the dominant roof, often so large that it accounts for half the height of the exterior elevation. Inside, its structure is exposed, sometimes revealing huge beams, over-sized for their function, that draw most of the interior interest. The roof's projecting eaves, which add grace and a sense of stability, can overhang as much as eight feet, extending the living space to the *engawa* or veranda below. With the removable walls, the deep eaves allow the house to be open on rainy days. They also shut out the high summer sun and admit the low rays of the winter sun. The *engawa* is a short step down from the living space and anchors the house to the land, making a shaded transition between indoor and outdoor space.

Anyone who has lived in a home built on a slab of concrete without a cellar can also appreciate the ancients' wisdom in elevating the floor of the Japanese house away from the cold and dampness. Since the occupants do not use furniture in the Western sense, but sit on the floor, the elevation is crucial to comfort. Floors are covered with two-and-a-half-inch thick reed mats, packed with straw and edged with fabric. Since the delicate mats, called *tatami,* are for sitting and sleeping, shoes are banned inside the house. The *tatami* are roughly 3 by 6 feet, and vary slightly in their dimensions according to locale. Rooms are measured by the number of mats that they contain; for example, "a 10-mat room" indicates its size. Where these *tatami* mats meet, the graphic lines of the fabric edging make a Mondrian-like composition and create the memorable geometric character of a Japanese room. What the casual observer may not realize, however, is that the unit of space represented by the *tatami* defines more than the flooring. This 3- by 6-foot module is also repeated on the walls and sliding doors, determining the positions of posts, windows and doors. All proportions are fixed and predictable, enabling traditional Japanese craftsmen to work on simple residences without elaborate blueprints. The module also facilitates design continuity in expanding the house as family size or fortune changes.

In a Japanese home, space is important for its emptiness. This emptiness can be equated with Japan's traditional philosophy that life is merely one phase in our total existence. The home is but a temporary shelter for the body while the soul tries to achieve enlightenment. It is not meant to be a showcase for materialism, although status used to be shown in such things as the number of ornaments on the roof's ridgepole. The serene interiors are achieved by putting almost everything out of sight in built-in cupboards. Prized possessions are rotated and displayed according to the season or the occasion and stored in a small outbuilding, called the *kura*, which is built to withstand fire, earthquake, climactic extremes and thieves.

Space is also considered an overture in the living experience. A room may be added at a slight distance from an existing room, so that in walking to it either through a hallway or an exterior covered passageway, one can see its exterior corners and have a feeling of inside-outside space.

Since the mathematical formula for the traditional Japanese house is so precise, one would expect that its interpretations as presented in this book would not be very diverse. However, as one homeowner pointed out, the results are like variations in classical music. Once the discipline is mastered, the interpretations are as rich and creative as the human mind can imagine. We hope you enjoy this special house tour made possible by so many individuals who graciously allowed us to share their vision. To them we extend our gratitude and our admiration for their perseverance in accomplishing their dreams.

"Our lack of formal training in Japanese architecture liberated us." Jim Marinaccio modestly analyzes how he and his wife, Marilyn, came to build two unique Japanese-style buildings near their house in New York's Hudson Valley.

The Marinaccios deal expertly in Japanese art at their Manhattan store, Naga Antiques. In the country they experiment, just as expertly, in Japanese construction. Jim continues, "What we have is a devotion to purity and form. And we respect the integrity of building materials and how they relate to the land."

The Marinaccios' 85 acres are a naturalist's delight, filled with wildlife, ancient trees, a picturesque pond that rushes noisily over a waterfall, and a profusion of flowers, both wild and cultivated. Wanting to participate more intimately in all this drama, the couple built a small teahouse a few hundred yards from their home. Tea, however, is the least of its pleasures. Since three of its walls can be totally removed, the structure invites camping out in high style and comfort. Often on a sultry night, the couple will sleep on *futons* on the floor, cooled by the sound of the waterfall and the night's breezes.

When the bedding is stowed behind sliding doors, as in Japan, a section of floor can be lifted to uncover a modern soaking tub for baths alfresco. The heated, filtered water, drawn from the pond, is unusually soft. On other occasions, and especially when the maples turn scarlet, the Marinaccios entertain one or two couples with a sunset *shabu shabu* dinner. The teahouse, or more accurately the *hanareya* (small, separate building), has its own miniscule kitchen and is even heated in winter.

Jim designed the versatile hide-away five years ago and had the wood — mostly cedar — forested and milled in Japan. He added several clever design solutions to carpenter Frank Ljutich's successful translation of Japanese style joinery. The insect screens, for example, can be removed and rolled up since they are edged by canvas, rather than a rigid frame, and are ingeniously clamped to the building like the tarp on a boat. In addition, canvas shades drop from the eaves in winter to protect the *shoji* screens with their laminated silk and paper panes.

The Marinaccios' other picturesque structure is a gazebo whose style Jim calls "Japanese Adirondack." Built on the foundation of an 18th-century sawmill, it offers the best view of the waterfall and dam which Jim patiently rebuilt, stone by stone.

Left: Like a prized antique resting on a small pedestal, a new East-West gazebo sits on the foundation of an old mill. A teahouse or *hanareya* hugs the slope.

Drawing its lines from two cultures, the gazebo is at home amid the rock formations, moss, ferns and tall pines.

"We derive a great deal of soul nourishment from this sort of living," Marilyn explains — which perhaps also explains why they were undaunted by the virtual jungle they inherited when they bought the property. Part of an old estate, the land had not been occupied since 1910. The main house and the carriage house had been sold off by the time the Marinaccios arrived in 1982, and a cluster of derelict buildings remained. Jim and Marilyn chose to convert the icehouse at the pond's edge into a weekend retreat "until we could build a big Tara up on the hill." Marilyn smiles remembering, "but now we realize that that would have been a mistake. We want to be as close to the water and all its wildlife as possible." The temporary quarters turned permanent and evolved into an appropriate setting for the couple's collection of Japanese, American and European country antiques.

"Our daughter, Maggie, is 13 now — she was four when we came here — and although she spends the week in the city, she has grown up here with the deer and the ducks, the possums and the woodchucks," Marilyn says. While Maggie tends her baby chicks and her show horse, Jim and Marilyn continue to tame the land and create a Monet-like border of perennials along the pond. "Moving the plants around satisfies our peripatetic natures," Marilyn reflects.

Years of traveling, particularly to Japan — and observing — have given the couple well-trained eyes, whether it's evaluating six-panel screens, their specialty for 20 years, or a piece of lumber. Jim is particularly appreciative of the Japanese use of cedar. In renovating the icehouse, he began using cedar from their land where it grows in abundance, but he preferred the fine, hand-planed and perfectly cylindrical cedar of Japan. On buying excursions through the Japanese countryside, he used to sketch the architecture of notable temples and houses he encountered. He didn't know why he did so at the time, but the process unquestionably served him well in designing the structures that have transformed neglected country property into an idyllic retreat.

The *hanareya*'s pillars rest on fieldstone "cushions," an ancient stabilizing technique against earthquakes. Ornamental grasses are used throughout the property as transition pieces to the natural woodland.

The round window, pride of craftsmen and inspiration of artists, takes a gourd form in the building's tiny kitchen. Marinaccio had his design custom-made in Japan.

The versatile *hanareya* can be used as a quiet hideaway, an inviting bathhouse or stylish guest quarters (turn page).

Right: Outside the *hanareya,* 17th-century Japanese monkeys, unusual in stone, not bronze, stand guard.

Below left: Inside, a 15th-century scholar's rock from China becomes a focal point for meditation.

Below right: Forest green takes on new meaning during a pleasant sylvan stroll to the structures.

Far right: The "Japanese Adirondack" gazebo is camouflaged by the lush woodland.

A bronze roof ornament, a status
symbol in old Japan, caps the
peak of the gazebo.

The sound and colors of summer
flood the spare shelter whose
posts are Japanese cedar.

He could have made his mark as a political scientist — perhaps a statesman — since his classical education, courtly manner and international business experience gave him a head start. Or he could have achieved wide fame as a writer, since his specialized books are gracefully expressed.

However, David H. Engel chose to put aside his doctoral studies in political science and instead became a landscape architect. He preferred to "save up in my head how one mountain masks another, how hills are contoured by trees, how streams eat away first one bank, then the other." Even as a boy in New Jersey he remembers noticing how gardens were put together, and, as he sat high in a favorite apple tree, made silent judgments about them. Today Engel's work in creating private, commercial and public gardens across the country has made him widely regarded as the leading American landscape architect trained in Japan. He is especially respected for his talent in rock composition.

Rocks are the most important feature of a Japanese garden since they bring all other components into relationship. Engel's hallmark is his use of boulders, rocks, pebbles and gravel in masterfully planned, but seemingly effortless, creations. "The Japanese garden is nature on a microcosmic scale," he explains. "This is not to say that it is nature imitated. Rather, it is nature symbolized." Rocks representing mountains, islands, waterfalls, seas and streams suggest the larger natural landscape no matter what size the garden. At the same time, they provide stark contrast — an essential component of Japanese design — to the textures and colors of the plantings.

Right: Written in stone, a stream designed by David H. Engel flows through a courtyard.

Engel's early travels after college took him to Tokyo in the 1950's where he "was bitten by the Japanese virus" that never left his system. He studied at Tokyo University of Fine Arts and then worked under Tansai Sano, the late master landscape architect of Kyoto.

On his return to the U.S., Engel, eager to share his new understanding, wrote a book, *Japanese Gardens for Today*, which brought him to the attention of Nelson Rockefeller, then Governor of New York, for whom he designed the now historic private garden in Pocantico Hills. His next two books, *A Japanese Touch for Your Garden* and *Creating a Chinese Garden*, helped thousands more readers understand Far Eastern gardening concepts.

Two recently created gardens exemplify many of the principles of Japanese garden design and Engel's artistic interpretations of them. The gardens also reflect the theme of another book he is preparing on his favorite subject, rocks, entitled *Bones of the Earth*. One garden is a romantic transformation of lakeside property; the other is actually two courtyard gardens that became an integral part of a new house.

LAKESIDE TRANSFORMATION

Bernice Stern and her late husband, Milton, had admired Engel's books for 20 years before they located him at his Manhattan office, Landgarden, to discuss their plans. The couple had just purchased a contemporary cedar home with Japanese architectural overtones to highlight their art, much of it Japanese, acquired in a lifetime of travel. They had been married 52 years when they found the four-year-old Connecticut home and were immediately drawn to its serene location overlooking a small lake. "This is my Shangri-la. I'm at peace with the world here," Mrs. Stern says, although her many philanthropic activities suggest that she is a bundle of energy. "After I lost my husband," she said, "I continued to develop the garden in his memory. Although he was a businessman, to his family he was a poet and an artist, and all our children share his sensibility for beauty."

In planning the Sterns' garden, Engel took his cue from the family's love of water and made its theme a rocky stream that appears to flow underneath the house to the larger garden behind. "The sound of water is as important as its visual impact," Engel explains. Although the lake was a ready source, local wetlands ordinances prevented drawing from it; therefore, two self-contained recirculating systems were engineered for front and back. Engel added a teak deck to link the land to the house and to provide a promontory over the sloping Eden.

A slightly Japanese bridge draws strollers to the lower level where the man-made plan segues into nature's handiwork at the lake's edge. To increase the apparent size of the garden, the focal point is placed as far as possible from the deck vantage point.

28

New England farmers built
fences with fieldstones.
David Engel fashioned them
into a stream where
there wasn't one.

Under the rocky bed, a
concrete sluiceway con-
tains the water in this
recirculating system.

Rich, cool and fragrant, a Japanese
garden reveals surprises at turns in the
path. "I love that feeling of mystery,"
Mrs. Stern confides. "One should
discover a garden step by step."

An existing Japanese maple shelters a new water garden by the front door. The stream, lined with oak-leaf hydrangea and water irises, turns the corner and appears to slip under the house.

Another home, farther north in Connecticut, offered a different opportunity for artful combinations of stone and plants. Working with the building's architect at the design stage, Engel flanked the entry with two gardens enclosed by stucco walls to match those of the eight-bedroom house. One of the two courtyards is symbolic in design; the

An imported water basin is artfully recessed into a bed of river stones to catch the overflow.

other, graced with tall Japanese cryptomeria, suggests a woodland. Five rooms open onto the courtyards, which hold more elements than are immediately visible to the eye. The secret lies in the interrelationships of the few components.

Two roads
can diverge
even in a
small wood,
magnifying
its size.

The woodland garden juxtaposes textures and colors. Irish moss is framed by granite and Mexican river stones.

The dry stream in the courtyard, executed by stonemason John De Riu, turns rubble fieldstone into a water mosaic.

Rocks covered with moss and lichens add color and the comfortable feeling of age.

The simulated stream glides out below the courtyard wall with fieldstone "wainscoting." One of the garden's shadblow trees makes an almost stylized contribution.

The shadblow or serviceberry tree adds height without mass. The first to bloom in late winter, it opens when shad run in the river. In fall, its leaves turn from green to yellow to red.

Chadine Flood Gong, an award-winning, California interior designer specializing in Japanese aesthetics, understood what her Palo Alto clients wanted. Involved with demanding professional careers, their children grown, the couple needed a new environment. Their 1970 Eichler-style house was ready for renovation and they hoped for a mix of Japanese quietude with a distinct sense of drama.

The clients had found Chadine, whose studio is in Los Gatos, through a magazine photo of one of her rooms, a minimalist sleeping alcove that matched their hopes. Seeing it, the wife uttered a mental "Eureka" and promptly engaged Chadine as both interior and landscape designer. Arthur Craig Steinman was selected as the project's architect.

When the renovation started, the front door opened onto a cement courtyard, an area that separates the two wings of the house and leads to the foyer. Chadine replaced the cement with a wooden deck and a narrow reflecting pool only four inches deep. The usual ornamental fish and plants were dismissed for ease of care, and the courtyard, accentuated by a lone black pine, is now a welcome sanctuary. Slate stepping stones across the pool also link the outdoor room to the master bedroom and contribute to the austere serenity.

Right: The courtyard designed by Chadine for low maintenance adds high drama and an air of serenity. The designer selects and places rocks with utmost care.

Since the husband's unpredictable schedule as a physician creates reading time in the middle of the night, a miniature *tatami* reading/sleeping alcove was designed off the master bedroom. Both the powder room and the master bath were also reconstructed into Japanese experiences, the latter enhanced by a small viewing garden just outside.

In addition, the couple was tired of ordinary kitchens and wanted an inviting "non-kitchen look" for both cooking and eating. Steinman raised the roof to add spaciousness, and Chadine combined red lacquered Italian cabinets with black granite counter tops for a polished, contemporary look.

Light pours into the kitchen, and another small Japanese garden is on view throughout the day.

Now, a year later, the house has been transformed so dramatically that the couple are reluctant to end the process. There are still more rooms and other outdoor areas for Chadine to redesign. And the owners, who have always appreciated California's climate after their Minnesota upbringing, doubly treasure their open-air home. "Chadine has made it a place we can't wait to come home to."

Entry gallery which connects the two wings of house is tiled with multi-colored African slate. The designer selected an antique Japanese screen with the same subtle colors as the slate.

Raised roof, glass wall and the absence of upper cabinets contribute to the kitchen's airiness. The range's hood was custom-made, purposely asymmetrical. A Japanese chest makes up for surrendered storage.

In the powder room, a Japanese chest is surmounted by a metal bowl for a wash basin. Its base has been cut out for the drain.

The fiberglass soaking tub, faced with slate, offers a view of the tiny walled garden that Chadine designed. The bamboo blinds, *sudare*, are one-way, allowing only a view out. A rain chain adds its graphics to the view.

Both rooms earned awards for excellence in design.

By day, it's a window
seat looking out to the
courtyard; by night, a
reading/sleeping
alcove almost under
the stars.

In the designer's home, a bath with a soaking tub faced with African slate became more Japanese with a *shoji* window treatment.

Chadine's own home has also undergone a room-by-room transformation. Even a small bathroom, which looks out on a eucalyptus tree planted to be viewed while bathing, has an Asian touch.

Downstairs, a *tatami* platform off the contemporary kitchen functions as an all-purpose family room. "We read here, relax, talk. I can add a low table for tea or Japanese-style dinners," Chadine points out. "My husband finds it the best place to feel at peace." The soft-spoken designer, a member of an aristocratic Thai family, a Fulbright scholar, and a former university professor of Asian Studies, finds time to translate academic books for publication and to write about Japanese gardens. She does her paperwork on the *tatami* at a portable Japanese table, acquired during her years of teaching in Japan. Overnight visitors discover the area a comfortable guest room, too, as they curl up on *futons* under the poetic shelter of a banana tree boldly painted on a rare screen.

This dismantable platform, covered with *tatami* mats in Chadine's home, is a modern version of the traditional tea ceremony room. It is a versatile stage set for reading, writing, dining, relaxing, even sleeping. Shoots of black bamboo, still green in their first year, rustle gently outside.

A bamboo "sleeve fence," named for its resemblance to a kimono's sleeves, unites the long, narrow garden with the house.

The designer painted her redwood house charcoal, eliminated deck railings and extended its interior serenity with a Japanese garden.

The winding, dirt road peters out to two tire tracks in the woods. Bushes close in as the trail twists up, obscuring the route and all chance of a view while driving up the mountain in California's Sonoma coastal range.

At the summit, *Yake-dono* appears. Taking its name from the Pomo Indian word for "our mountain," *Yake-dono* is the weekend refuge of three San Francisco businessmen, Delwin Rimbey, Steve Fletcher and Carl Croft. Its 360-degree view is incomparable... sunrise, sunset, a starry dome at night, and a display of nature's majesty all day long.

The three partners bought the land in 1975 and were content at first to camp out on the peak before they built a small cabin. But in 1978 a raging forest fire leveled the structure and much of their 42 acres. Discouraged but not defeated, the trio had to wait several more years before they could rebuild. This time, it would be a Japanese-style house, inspired by those seen on buying trips to Japan for Tampopo, their wholesale business of traditional arts and crafts, and for Dandelion, their general gift and bookstore in San Francisco.

"We wanted a house where we could feel the outdoors and smell its seasons as we did camping," Rimbey said. "We wanted to be in continual touch with the natural beauty around us." The initial inspiration for the building came

from a favorite teahouse in the gardens of the Katsura Imperial Villa, the famous 17th-century estate near Kyoto. Guided by personal photographs and on-site drawings, as well as a collection of books on Japanese architecture, the three partners worked out a floor plan for their weekend home. Since the exposed site on the mountain top dictated a massive style, the design evolved into a structure more akin to the open plan of the traditional Japanese farmhouse or *minka*, rather than a teahouse. From the detailed drawings and elevations, Rimbey constructed a wooden scale model of the proposed structure, which permitted the owners to refine their plans and resolve such interior considerations as functional cabinetry.

A local builder, Julian Curran, was selected as collaborator, but before his

Yake-dono stands alone, an East/West house with an Indian name and three owners whose avocation became construction. The log beams have hammered copper end covers.

arrival, Croft, Fletcher and Rimbey excavated and built the 20,000-gallon cistern for the house's water supply. Curran then selected three Douglas fir trees from a nearby forest to become the principal horizontal beams of the timber frame dwelling. The huge logs were prepared and finished on the ground in advance along with all the other principal timbers for the framing, as is the tradition in Japanese joinery.

After two months of preparation, the components were lifted into place by a crane in a few short hours to form the "bones" of the structure. A traditional Japanese clay tile roof was installed by Ted Chida. Enduring and fire resistant, the tile was an ideal choice for the area frequently threatened by forest fire.

The main structure of living area, kitchen, bath and loft was completed in 1986. The living area is extended by a commanding deck on the eastern facade and a narrow deck on two others. Comfortable chairs wait outside; inside, a low Japanese dining table concedes to Western comfort with a deep recess beneath. Glass sliding doors allow the interior space to be open on three sides to the great outdoors.

The central fireplace, working overtime, separates the kitchen from the rest of the house, which is appointed with country antiques. Even the unique refrigerator looks curiously Japanese. An undersized model designed for a recreational vehicle, it is wedged snugly into the back of a staircase chest and is faced with a reed shade.

Since it is perched far beyond the reach of public utility lines, the house has its own electric generator and solar power. The area is so remote that at night lights can be seen twinkling across the range nearly 60 miles away.

Six years after completing the central house, the men added "The Annex," a wing of three generous bedrooms and a library, under the supervision of a friend and retired contractor John Kroo. This time the structure was influenced by another 17th-century Kyoto villa, the hillside retreat Shisendo, built by the Japanese aesthete Ishikawa Jozan. The wing's ground floor bedrooms are modeled on the scenery-viewing room of the villa, as is its upper level, designed for a vista of the gardens and for moon-viewing. The annex, reached by a covered, transitional walkway that zigzags past a courtyard garden and a lap pool, sits apart yet is solidly tied to the original house.

Far left: The narrow deck, modeled after the transition verandas of old Japan, looks west and north.

Above: Local Douglas fir supplies warm tones to the organic roof and loft.

Left: The timber frame was finished on the ground and erected in a day.

Night gives way to dawn in the remote mountaintop retreat, where candlelight is a frequent reminder to "slow down." The two-piece Japanese staircase chest to the loft is recessed into the exterior wall for a built-in look.

Antique
lanterns, part
of a varied
collection,
appoint the
entryways.

A water basin, originally intended
to purify hands and heart before
the tea ceremony, is nestled near
the entry. The bamboo lantern is
contemporary.

Helga and Phillip Fleishman's home is cut into the California hillside, cantilevered out to capture the maximum view of the San Francisco skyline across the bay and the cluster of sailboats moored by the near shore. The vessels, if not luring the viewer to a leisurely sail, form a constantly changing watercolor for contemplation.

The area once housed many sea captains who prized the location for its link with the sea, and it became a repository for treasures brought back from their long voyages, especially from the Orient. In 1975, the Fleishmans decided it was a natural neighborhood to launch Imari Inc., a business in Japanese antiques. As the gallery grew in their home, living space dwindled, and they decided to look for another house nearby that would provide the same dramatic panorama. Farther up the hill, they found an undistinguished three-bedroom tract house with a similar view and a Japanese garden. The garden was the deciding factor. They bought the house with a resolve to renovate.

Their goal was to duplicate the serenity of their previous quarters where they were surrounded by fine Japanese art, especially screens. They decided to throw open their walls to the outside, Japanese style, and extend their living and dining space with a narrow deck like the *engawa* that connects Japanese rooms to the exterior. Most important, the Fleishmans decided to strip the rooms of clutter and allow their rich and changing collection of art to draw all interior attention.

In 1988, Phillip invited one of California's recognized authorities on Japanese architecture, Len Brackett, to head the renovation. He created an intricate interior ceiling that elicits gasps of appreciation from many visitors, who often tend to whisper in admiration at the Japanese joinery. Says Helga, "Usually they fall immediately in love with the woodwork. However," she continues with a smile, "a few are bewildered by the emptiness of the rooms, and ask if we have just moved in."

The interior is not empty, but filled with tranquility, which was the hallmark of the late Marc Miyasato, whom Phillip says "understood more than most

Right: With most of the glass sliders removed from this California hillside house, the outside comes in. Seemingly detached from its moorings, it takes on an ethereal quality. The temple railing, generous roof overhang and Japanese rainchain extend the design theme.

Adorned only by warm tones and
graphic angles, the entry stairway
prepares visitors for the natural,
organic harmony that awaits.

designers how to satisfy today's need for quietude." The family never tires of the warm woods and the flexibility of the easy, functional space. Their son, Michael, and his teen-aged friends particularly like the openness and the freedom it brings.

All of the cedar pieces were hand-planed at Brackett's East Wind Inc. headquarters in the foothills of the Sierras and then fitted together at the house without visible nails like a giant puzzle. Port Orford, an especially fragrant cedar, and western red cedar are the principal woods, along with some Japanese *keyaki* (zelkova) and sugar pine.

Brackett's glass sliders are also made from hand-hewn and hand-planed cedar which, like much of the construction, needs no further finishing, neither sanding nor oiling. The wood is allowed to enjoy a life cycle of its own as it mellows, weathers, even cracks gracefully into a rich old age. The one exception is the maple flooring, which has been covered with a non-yellowing urethane.

The Fleishmans' road to serene interiors started with a fascination for just the opposite. As a teen-ager on vacation in Britain, Helga was impressed by the enormous Imari porcelains in lavish country houses and castles. "Those magnificent platters with exotic figures in foreign lands stirred my imagination and longing to travel." Her initial career took her on frequent trips to Japan where she began to buy the china that launched their Sausalito business.

"Obviously," Helga continues, "I have travelled a long way aesthetically from admiring palatial rooms filled with splendid porcelains, rich carpets, gold and silver, to preferring simplicity and the relative lack of ornamentation found in traditional Japanese design. The display of one scroll or screen in a spare, but finely crafted room is pleasing to me now. Japanese art is endlessly fascinating because I will never know it all. In its simplicity and abstraction, it is more complex, challenging and satisfying than the baroque and roccoco of my own Austria."

A serenely understated interior plays counterpoint to an intricate cedar ceiling. The rare 18th-century six-panel screen competes with a compelling view across San Francisco Bay.

The family room, stripped down to bare essentials,
conveys immediate calm. The requisite TV is subdued
in the Japanese chest. The unassuming antiques
include a sea chest, a *ranma* (interior transom) turned
into a coffee table by Price Crozer, and a sign for
tooth blackening powder over the fire.

California craftsman Bill Eichenberger combined the rich grains of oak and zelkova, the wood used for most Japanese chests, to build a staircase chest to the bedrooms. Square bamboo forms the handrail.

Antique tea ceremony baskets, bamboo's gift to art, are admired for their natural beauty and simplicity. The small one is a lined tea caddy, signed by a master.

Luminous front doors and strategically located windows allow the garden's greenery to color the entryway. The cupboard, a standard fixture in Japan to conceal shoes and slippers, is rendered here in Port Orford and western red cedar.

When Richard and Linda Reitzes' architect saw their proposed building site bordering a rushing stream, he said, "I'd like to design a house that would rest lightly on the earth like an insect." His simile was apt since the Reitzes did not want to tame their 17-acre homesite, a rolling woodland in New York's Harlem Valley. They wanted to disturb it as little as possible in order to "bond with the beauty of the land."

Their recently completed country home is the product of years of preparation, first to find a secluded and beautiful site within a two-hour drive from New York City, and then to locate an architect who could actualize their hopes. Since the couple admire Japan's literature, theater and especially its architecture, their prerequisite was a low maintenance dwelling with distinctly Japanese features. After finding an ideal location on the New York/Connecticut border, they came across the right architect quite by chance while on vacation in North Carolina. Driving through the Nags Head Conservancy on the Outer Banks, they noticed two wood-framed buildings with the pleasing proportions and simplicity they had in mind. Locating the architect, Joe Sam Queen, in Waynesville, North Carolina, they invited him to consider their building site. After his spontaneous enthusiasm, the three pored over books illustrating Japanese architecture to arrive at a concept. It took a year of development and several design versions to reach consensus.

Cost was the next, almost insurmountable, obstacle. When construction firms were contacted, the Reitzes were shocked to see that the proposed figures for their two-bedroom house were more than double their original budget. After

Right: At the end of a long road, a brand new country home settles into the woods.

a few weeks of emotional reassessment, they reconsidered the plans. Approximately 250 sq. feet of the 2,500-square-foot structure were readily eliminated, some structural designs were altered, as were certain building material specifications. The biggest cost reduction, however, was achieved by Richard's taking on the role of general contractor. He put in hundreds of hours after work on the fax and phone and thousands of miles in travel to hire individual craftsmen and find the best materials at the lowest cost.

The final product is a Japanese-style house that lets the Reitzes feel part of

the continual cycle of renewal outside and holds high tech comforts within: gleaming European kitchen appliances, sleek bathroom fixtures, central air conditioning, and double-paned window walls in the principal rooms.

The house is designed in a "U" shape with the wings connected by a generous front foyer. The kitchen, dining and living rooms are on one side; the bedrooms with adjoining baths, on the other. The bedrooms have traditional Japanese *tatami* mats recessed into clear-stained Douglas fir flooring with queen-sized *futon*s from the Manhattan shop, Five Eggs. A Zen rock garden fills the expanse between the two wings, which on many nights is bathed in the moon's soft light.   Three-foot decks or walkways, covered by the roof's overhang, flank the rock garden and wrap around two sides of the house, affording views of the stream's little waterfalls.

The stream, a dominant feature of the landscape in winter, twists down towards the house and sparkles past, below a deck. The house is sited so that the stream is the compelling focal point of the living room's view. The Rietzes, like so many people drawn to Japanese architecture, have a natural affinity for wood.   Twenty years ago, they started collecting African art, partly for its fragrant wood and partly

from their natural preference for purity of line, the same quality found in many forms of Japanese art which they later began to acquire.

Richard believes that the momentum of building will make it difficult for him to stop, so he hopes to direct his expertise to a new avocation: advising others on building Japanese-style dream houses.

The house is elevated from the dampness like its ancient predecessors. Its laterally applied clear cedar siding is still unweathered.

Rather than divert the stream and an ancient fieldstone wall, the house accommodates them.

Far left: In the meditative court-yard, stones used as brush strokes produce a composition akin to the black ink paintings of China and Japan.

Left: Afternoon sun spotlights details — grade A cedar planks fastened with blind nails; beveled railing, inspired by a photograph of a Japanese house; Marvin sliders of ponderosa pine.

Below: *Shoji* screens, supplied by Miya Shoji, are made of bass-wood, a stable, light colored and lightweight linden.

To some, the John P. Humes Japanese Stroll Garden may simply be a walk in the woods. To others, according to Stephen Morrell, "It is a lesson in learning to deal with life, as it unfolds one step at a time."

The difference in awareness often is cultural. "Westerners sometimes look without seeing," says Morrell, Western himself and curator of the four unusual acres in Mill Neck, New York. He is also a dedicated student of Zen Buddhism.

Morrell leads the way along a shaded path, explaining the sights. His distinguished credentials seem at odds with his youthful appearance: landscape designer, lecturer, author, instructor at both the New York and Brooklyn Botanical Gardens in addition to Stroll Garden curator.

The garden, he explains, was originally the inspiration of an American diplomat, John P. Humes, who traveled in the Far East in the 1950's and wanted to create an idyllic corner on his Long Island estate. Working with Japanese designers, Humes completed the project in 1962 and ornamented the two-acre garden with an imported teahouse.

Later, during Humes' assignment as ambassador to Austria, the garden became neglected and overgrown, and in 1980, the Humes Foundation invited Morrell to take charge. Morrell decided to expand the site into a stroll garden for passive recreation and contemplation. "A garden should be an intimate experience. My hope is to create a sense of paradise where man and nature are in harmony." Buddhism, he reminds, believes that children are perfect and complete. "As children we lack nothing and have an awareness of paradise that fades with the conditioning of life. Meditation should allow us to return to spontaneous insights and not be influenced by our preconceptions."

Right: Turns in the path at the John P. Humes Stroll Garden purposely conceal its course.

The route Morrell created in the Stroll Garden represents a journey along the road to wisdom. The first gate, a stylized version of the *torii* found at Japanese temples, marks the transition from worldly activity. The turns in the path purposely conceal its course, so the stroller can immerse himself in the sights at hand and deal with them one step at a time. "One must meander like the stepping stones," Morrell advises, "and not be goal-oriented. Otherwise, the experience is lost."

The path broadens in richer sections to call attention to the plants and stones, grouped like artful still lifes of muted greens and yellows with contrasting leaf sizes and textures. The walkway narrows to hasten steps through limited terrain. Openings in the paths encourage strollers to pause and see the view. Other components also control the experience. An expanse of moss, for example, defines open space to draw the eye towards a grouping of plants or stones that edge it. "The eye is naturally drawn to open space, just the way a plant is pulled towards the sun," Morrell says. The moss works like an arrow to highlight the dramatic grouping.

In the garden, American and Japanese versions of the same species thrive side by side. Pachysandra, the evergreen ground cover so familiar to Americans, turns out to be the Asian variety; its less common American cousin is deciduous.

The opening route ascends to represent climbing a mountain, symbol of sacred space and source of enlightenment. On the downward slope, the mulched path changes into white gravel, suggesting water emerging from the mountain peak. "Water represents our pure beginnings as children," continues Morrell, a born teacher. "And just as waters course through smooth and difficult sections along the way, we go through joyful and troublesome experiences on our journeys to enlightenment. Instead of seeing ourselves as separate from other people, we must understand that we have an interdependence with all things."

By the time the path reaches the second gate, the visitor has been encouraged by the garden's design to recapture his birthright awareness and its absence of bias. "Each moment needs to be accepted as it occurs and not judged." The white gravel continues its downward course, mimicking how a stream moves in nature, and finally flows into a pond symbolizing the ocean which receives streams and makes them one. Filled with an awareness of oneness and unity, the stroller passes through the final gate back to the world, prepared to apply the lessons of the garden to his life, and hoping to improve each day. The teahouse offers a final experience, first of humility in bowing low to enter, and then joy of friendship with shared tea, whose bright green color also symbolizes new life, new beginnings.

Right above: A water basin nestles amid a tapestry of textures and greens, selected for their contrasting leaf size.

Right below: A rustic crossing spans a river of moss.

Moss gives a sense of age and is key in connecting components.

Right: A third gate leads to the pilgrim's goal or shrine, in this instance, a teahouse imported from Japan.

Far right: A rocky shoreline is artfully rendered in black stone.

The painting on the sliding
doors depicts the experi-
ence of the wayfarer
approaching the mountain
of enlightenment.

Seen through a screen, a
weeping hemlock and a
cutleaf maple contrast with
a mugho pine, severely
pruned to look windswept.
The stone lantern extends
the architecture of the teahouse into the garden.

A Zen garden liberates the mind from Manhattan's visual overload, extending the color and minimal style of the three-story atrium. Walls are capped with copper.

Right: The trees, three columnar hornbeams, chosen because of their narrow, upright pattern of growth, are softened at their base by liriope, a shade-loving, grass-like evergreen. Morrell framed the edge with blue stone to give the small plot depth.

Stephen Morrell's interpretations of Zen philosophy are not limited to the Humes Stroll Garden. Three very different examples of his design work for private gardens reveal the breadth of possibilities.

One garden is found behind a Manhattan brownstone with a soaring three-story atrium. Its owner, an international executive who lived for a time in the Far East, turned down a succession of landscapers' plans for conventional flower gardens. He realized that his fast-paced lifestyle warranted a calming escape from the bustling city. He needed a Zen-like extension of the atrium's serene interior. "After talking five minutes with Morrell, I knew I had the right man," the owner recalled. "He understood exactly what I wanted and from then on I didn't have to think about it." Composed essentially of three horizontal rocks and three vertical trees on a background of white gravel, the garden continues the minimal, all-white theme of the interior designed by George Dandridge "I love its simplicity," the executive said, "and its quiet, meditative, utterly peaceful feeling."

ECHOING THE VIEW

Over the years, Doris and Thomas Ackerman's preference in
gardens have run the gamut — from formal flower beds
and extensive lawns to roses and wildflowers. But after visiting the Japanese gardens in Kyoto, and then the Humes
Japanese Stroll Garden in Mill Neck, Doris found her real
love. Her admiration for Morrell's work led to his creation of
a meditation garden for her home overlooking Cold Spring

Harbor, New York. Working on a plateau above the Ackerman house, Morrell created a grouping of stones and plantings to echo the view: the undulating hills across the harbor, the expanse of water, the hill up to the house, even the gravel drive that borders the garden. The ideal, Morrell says, is to find harmony between site, garden and the home owner's wishes. Doris tied the bamboo fence herself and encouraged the moss to spread after moving it from the hillside. "Weeding and pruning," she says with a smile, "are my meditation."

This undulating grouping, which echoes the site and the view, invites repose and the feeling of being one with the universe.

A third garden at a Connecticut home indicates how Japanese design principles can work to link two structures. The owners had added a carriage house/office to their property, close to their Greek Revival-style home. Morrell was invited to unite the two buildings visually. Work began with a wooden wall to reflect the Greek Revival architecture and form a backdrop for the garden. An upright Japanese maple was planted in front of the fence as a focal point. The tree was selected to create a relationship in texture and form with existing maples beyond the fence. Low growing shrubs were planted in a curving "L" shape beneath the maple, interspersed with richly grained stones that move the eye along the expanse.

A graceful swath of gravel repeats the curve and is, in turn, repeated by a border of river stones along the house. This alternating perspective of wide and narrow exemplifies, Morrell points out, the *yin* and *yang* principle of Oriental philosophy, the harmony of complementary contrasts.

In another part of the garden, a short path of stone and granite slabs, quintessentially Japanese, accords readily with the new Greek Revival colonnade that marks the path to the carriage house.

Right: Greek columns line the walkway from the Greek Revival-style house past the Japanese garden.

Left: Old mill stones harmonize with the rectangular shapes of the path and the Japanese-inspired water basin.

Right: Azalea, dwarf barberry and mugho pine under the Japanese maple are set off by a native local ground cover, bearberry. The ornamental grass at right is northern sea oats.

Below: The line created by the stones is enhanced by the undulating contours of the plantings and is repeated in the sweep of gravel "sea" and stone borders. The black river stones are embedded in dyed concrete.

When Yuki and Gene Danaher lead the way to the dining room in their Manhattan apartment, first-time guests are unprepared for the remarkable sight that awaits. A full-sized teahouse, walled with *shoji* screens and resting on a platform, occupies a third of the room. Constructed on a diagonal in a rear corner of their vaulted 100-year-old loft, it invites rather than intrudes.

The dining room teahouse solved several design problems for the Danahers in their spacious (2,800 square feet) apartment. The previous owners had used the back portion of the loft as a combination bedroom, study and sitting area. The Danahers preferred to make the space a dining room, but in so doing, forfeited the guest room and created an awkwardly large dining area. The teahouse, designed by Hisao Hanafusa, owner of Miya Shoji Interiors, provided an imaginative solution. It created pleasant guest quarters insulated from street noise; it reduced the dining space to more compact dimensions; and it added visual interest and balance, since its *shoji* screens matched those used on the opposite wall to conceal a narrow study.

The Danahers were initially drawn to their top floor loft by its space, light and overall fine craftsmanship. The previous owners, working with architects Douglas Peix and William Crawford, had renovated it to be a showcase for their modern art collection. Skylights flood the living areas with sun and underline the rich tones of the wooden floors.

Right: The soaring stairway is crowned with a stained glass window depicting flowing obis. The teahouse stands below on the right.

A wide unconventional stairway is the architectural centerpiece in the living area and leads up to a sitting area and rear terrace. The Danahers added a stained glass expanse at the top of the stairway that suggests billowing obis, the luxurious sashes worn with kimonos. Marie-Pascale Foucalt, an artisan at a nearby studio, created the final design based on Gene's rough drawings.

The Danaher's six-sided tearoom, small by Japanese standards with its three-and-a-half *tatami* mat layout, is quite likely the only one of its kind in existence. In order not to encroach on the dining area with a square corner, Hanafusa created the unusual floorplan. The tearoom's recessed lighting and oversized *tokonoma* (display alcove), located at the farthest point from the dining table, create an illusion of depth. Its raised base suggests outside space, so that

Guests are delighted with the
ambiance created by a custom-
made teahouse tucked in the corner
of a Manhattan loft.

The teahouse also doubles as a private guest room. Drawers in the floor's base hold the *futon* bedding.

Opposite the teahouse,
a wall of sliding *shoji*
instantly erases a study's
necessary clutter.

diners can feel they are outdoors near a teahouse. A small rock garden at the base of the teahouse furthers this suggestion.

The lightweight *shoji* frames are made of sturdy basswood, a kind of linden which resists expansion and contraction. The panes are plastic-coated paper, which are easier to clean and less fragile than traditional *washi* paper.

Although devoid of furniture, the classic tearoom is not bare. Reflecting Japan's great talent for precision and harmony, its clean lines convey restfulness. A finished tearoom is rather like a fine cabinet in its craftsmanship, yet its unsophisticated components — such as bamboo ceilings, straw-matted flooring and muted walls — are intended to affirm man's oneness with nature.

The teahouse is also a manifestation of both Danahers' appreciation of Japan and the tea ceremony. Gene's interest in having a strong Japanese element in his home stems from his studies in Japan. He earned a Masters degree in Japanese law at Tokyo University and was the first Westerner in the history of the school to write a dissertation in Japanese. Yuki's appreciation for authentic tea ceremony settings began as a girl in Japan where for many years she studied *Chado*, the Way of Tea.

The tea ceremony itself is more relaxing interlude than ceremonial occasion. In ancient Japan, tea was thought to offer medicinal as well as mystical benefits by cleansing the body and purifying the mind. To serve and share tea are still considered a manifestation of humility and a celebration of friendship. Guests are supposed to praise the art displayed in the minimal surroundings as well as the objects used in the tea service, especially the handmade tea bowls, often the ultimate expression of the Japanese potter's art. Participants should also mentally admire the gracefulness of the host or hostess's preparation and presentation of the tea. Everyone's movements, even the guests, follow a prescribed pattern. Other conversation is inappropriate, and all cares are supposed to be left outside the teahouse in order to find a degree of inner peace.

With the teahouse providing a ready escape from New York's dynamics within their own four walls, the Danahers can draw on the best of both worlds.

While many Manhattanites rejoice at not having a lawn to tend, one New Yorker delights in devoting his leisure time to a 1,000-square-foot patch of land behind his townhouse. There he has created a private sanctuary with a miniature Japanese garden, complete with teahouse.

On view through the glass wall of the dining room, the garden offers a sense of lush refreshment that far exceeds its size. His wife takes particular delight in its decorative contribution to the interior, furnished with a quiet blend of European and Japanese antiques.

Undaunted by first having had to conquer a fungus in the soil, the executive/gardener has succeeded in cultivating a variety of plants, including the esoteric Himalayan plant scarcofogus and some which traditionally ornament a Japanese garden — bamboo, mugho pine and Coral Bark maple. Other plants are indigenous to the region, such as crab apple and ailanthus, described by the owner as a "New York junk tree," the species memorialized in the book, *A Tree Grows in Brooklyn.*

A tiny backyard garden leading to a teahouse outshines a splendid antique screen in its seasonal displays.

The garden is the culmination of considerable research, its owner having drawn inspiration from the masterful creations he saw on frequent trips to Japan. To define his own idea of a Japanese garden, he studied with two masters and took lessons in *bonsai* (the art of growing dwarf trees in shallow containers) from a third who was Emperor Hirohito's *bonsai* master.

In spite of its size, the garden holds a surprising number of traditional features, among them a waterfall, a bridge, a water basin, two lanterns, fossilized rocks, a heated carp pool, and at the end of the path, the teahouse. There in the intimate enclosure, garden scents mingle with those of *tatami* and the fragrant wood used in its construction. Built by Japanese craftsmen, the teahouse is just four *tatami* mats big. In ancient Japan, the first space assigned in private homes for the tea ceremony was four and a half mats — about nine feet square. According to Arthur Drexler in *The Architecture of Japan*, "This was the amount of space in which a legendary

Buddhist figure received a saint and his 86,000 disciples in a demonstration of the non-existence of space to the truly enlightened." Drexler adds that a Chinese philosopher declared, "The true reality of a room was not its walls, but the emptiness they contained."

The Manhattan couple, however, prefer to think of their teahouse as a stage set for the human drama, using it for tête à têtes, small lunches or dinners.

The first independent teahouse was created late in the 16th century by Sen-no-Rikyu, the teamaster from whom the Urasenke School of Tea takes its origins. He made the approach through the garden an integral part of its design, and landscaped the path to distract guests from all thoughts of the outside world. Recreated here 400 years later, this luxuriant retreat provides the same release amid the skyscrapers of Manhattan.

Right: In the teahouse, *shoji* screens can be arranged to frame portions of the view, like changing paintings on display. Astilbe brighten the entrance.

Far right: The garden defines the dining room. The stone tray on the dining table holds spirit stones, handsome geological specimens.

The front entrance of the Kehoe home is enclosed, yet open, creating ideal transition space. The rock/lantern at right comes from Japan.

Three thousand miles away on the Pacific Coast, another small garden demonstrates the power of the miniscule and the architectural role of Japanese gardens. Barbara and Robert Kehoe, owners of a San Francisco business in Japanese antiques, the Robert Brian Company, designed their California ranch-style home with an interior courtyard that is a private setting for the interplay of sunlight and shadow, soft greens and glistening stone.

Japanese gardens are to be admired for their line and mass rather than color, and generally depend on a subdued palette of greens and greys with only occasional short-lived bursts of blooms in the spring and autumn. Symmetry is always avoided since it is not only considered opposed to nature, it stifles imagination. Asymmetry forces each viewer to have a unique experience, to complete the picture mentally.

Enclosed by a redwood fence, the Kehoe garden functions as an additional room that suffuses the adjacent living room and foyer with beauty. Unlike Western

A California residential garden has been sprinkled with water to evoke the fresh sweetness that follows a rain.

design, where the house becomes part of the landscape, a Japanese garden, integrated with the dwelling by fencing, becomes part of the house. Its components, scaled to the interior, are part of its symbolic vocabulary of suggestion. In Japanese art, water in its many forms — rain, snow, fog, cloud and ice — has always been a device for contemplation of the universe. The dry stream of river stones, interspersed with water-loving irises to intensify the suggestion, represents infinity.

Stone lanterns originated on temple grounds to hold fire, the sacred symbol of life, and were later adopted for the tea garden. They have come to represent the five elements of the universe in ancient Japanese cosmology — sky, wind, fire, water and earth.

California landscaper Wayne Kikuchi designed the Kehoe garden, using a lacy Japanese maple, azaleas, a flowering quince, mugho pines, nandina and corokia. Ground covers of Green Carpet and Corsican Mint complete the scene.

A day with Len Brackett in the foothills of the Sierras is more than a visit; it is a pilgrimage. Trees are his passion, his life, his cause. Yet even though he lives and works high in a national forest that is virtually inaccessible three months of the year, Brackett is not a remote guru. Relaxed and conversational like an old friend not seen in years, he is immediately interesting.

Brackett, whose company, East Wind (*Higashi Kaze*), Inc., specializes in the building of custom-made Japanese houses, cares more about wood and knows more about wood than one would think possible. His career began with five arduous years as an apprentice to a master temple carpenter in Kyoto. "Japanese carpentry," he says, "can only be studied, never mastered. Before I went to Japan, I could never have guessed at the complexity of Japanese carpentry techniques nor the depth of knowledge and tradition tied to it."

Brackett stresses that even now, 17 years after returning from Japan, he is not an architect in the Western sense of the word, nor a master carpenter by Japanese standards, a recognition accorded to only about 10 men after decades of experience. His training is based on an ancient system of complex grid patterns and geometric proportions developed and passed down by Japanese master craftsmen. Brackett views himself "as a very new, continually learning Western link in a very old and continuous chain."

Having benefited from so much intense teaching and kindness in Japan, Brackett feels a personal obligation to pass on to the next generation a portion of the cumulative knowledge of 1,500 years of Japanese carpentry. He is surrounded by a dedicated staff of college-educated young Americans who share his devotion to fine craftsmanship and its continuation.

As Chairman of the Forest Resource Committee of the Timber Framer's Guild of North America, he is also committed to the fight to stop the destructive logging depleting the rich forests of the west, which he describes as "the last great temperate softwood forests in the world."

Returning to California in 1976, Brackett took two and a half years to build his own home above Nevada City, five miles from the nearest power hookup.

Right: Nestled in one of the world's richest forests, this quintessential Japanese house, painstakingly built by Len Brackett, uses American materials for all its principal parts, many from the site itself.

Working with only one helper, his first apprentice Walter Hardzog, he created a classic Japanese dwelling and a rare U.S. example of ancient architectural woodworking techniques. While the work was in progress, Brackett camped on the site for six months with his wife, Toshiko, and their baby son, Sylvan. In typical pioneer spirit, when he needed help hoisting the timber frame into place, he rallied 25 sturdy neighbors, some of them foresters, to do it all in a day.

Brackett is among a select group of American craftsmen who, on their own, have apprenticed in Japan. He was fortunate in being able to work under Hide Tadayuki, Mitsuji Yoshihisa and Hosomi Tadaki, all premier temple carpenters and among the top one percent of the country's wood craftsmen. During his first two years as apprentice in Kyoto, he was permitted only to hand plane boards and timbers, a skill virtually unknown to American carpenters. He worked 12 hours a day, seven days a week with one day off every two weeks to study and care for his tools.

The Japanese plane, which is pulled along the wood rather than pushed like the Western version, is capable of shaving a curl 2/1000 of an

inch thin. When the wood is planed correctly, it is as smooth as glass, and no further finishing is necessary. The Japanese rarely finish traditional architectural woodwork with sealer except portions of temples and shrines. Because of the smooth razor cut of the fibers, there are no tiny hairs or broken grain. The wood is microscopically smooth and glows with cleanly reflected light, creating a warm richness unattainable in stained or varnished wood. Wood subjected to sanding — even with very fine sandpaper — scatters light. Sanded wood also picks up dirt if it's left unsealed, and its grain may eventually raise. The grain in wood that has been hand planed properly will not raise even if it gets soaking wet.

Brackett's custom Japanese homes in the U.S., constructed mainly with local materials, demonstrate the richness of ancient techniques and have drawn considerable attention in national publications on building. However, having satisfied his purist soul by constructing his own home without yielding to conventional Western comforts, Brackett now combines these techniques with Western technologies that do not compromise the buildings' aesthetics — insulation, air-conditioning, Western kitchens — to

The courtyard garden is on view from every room except the American kitchen. The house has 104 removable sliding doors, each made of fragrant Port Orford cedar, each hand-planed to a glassy luster without stain or varnish.

make the structures more practical and affordable. Two of these homes, one in Tiburon, California, and one in Hawaii are shown in this chapter along with Brackett's own home.

Since Japanese builders plot their structures on a fixed unit, the dimensions of a *tatami* mat, roughly 3 by 6 feet, Brackett's buildings are designed in the same fashion. In order to help clients assess their spatial needs, he presents them with a box of dominoes and asks them to make miniature floor plans with them, since dominoes have the same proportions as *tatami.*

Once the plan is made, much of the construction work is done in the East Wind shop located 200 yards up the hill from Brackett's house. The location is near what Brackett rates as some of the last great stands of timber in the world: first- and second-growth sugar pine, ponderosa pine, incense cedar. With these woods plus western red cedar and the rare Port Orford cedar obtained from the Northwest Coast, he has the essential woods for Japanese-style construction. Since the houses are timber-framed, much of the work can be done in advance and then assembled in a few days at a distant site. All framing timber, the interior structure for the roof, *shoji*, windows, even Brackett's patented light fixtures are prepared by hand at East Wind and hand planed. Everything is jointed, including the ceiling moldings, and then fitted together at the final location, like a gigantic puzzle. The pieces are pounded together with heavy wooden mallets, generally without the use of nails.

Outside the shop, timber is air-dried three to five years in covered stacks. Wood that won't shrink is key to making joints that won't open. The fragrant Port Orford cedar is Brackett's favorite because it is stable, straight-grained, rot resistant, beautiful and very strong. Without a finish, its fragrance will last forever. Most of the U.S.'s limited supply is exported to Japan, where it is used for temple and shrine building.

Brackett's early days as an Oregon logger, while a student at Reed College, put him in touch with lumberjacks all along the West Coast who call him when they have superb specimens. The finds are sometimes extremely rare: recently he traded a ten-wheeler flat bed truck for a truckload of California nutmeg, a member of the redwood family favored in Japan for *Go* game boards, playing boards that sell for thousands of dollars. When the lumber at East Wind is dry, it is cut

Cattail reeds from the yard make the window's grid. The walls are a mix of mud and straw applied over cedar laths and then stuccoed.

into required dimensions. Boards are numbered as they come off the saw so that grain patterns match when the boards are installed. Brackett explains that while many homes in the United States show the influence of Japanese architecture, they are basically American houses

Every traditional home includes a *tokonoma*, a display alcove for scrolls and seasonal flower arrangements.

that have had Japanese elements added to them. "We do the opposite. We start with a Japanese house and change it to reflect an American lifestyle. This way the elements that are crucial to a genuine Japanese house — the timber frame and its proportional elements, the natural materials and the traditional finishes — are integral parts of the structure."

Brackett's son, Sylvan, is a teen-ager now, as is his second child, daughter Aya. Although they are at home in their almost primeval surroundings in the Sierra foothills, summers in Kyoto have made them cosmopolitan as well and have perhaps given them the perspective to realize that they too can be part of the ancient chain.

In a Brackett-built house in Tiburon, California, a typical Japanese entryway with a bench step for removal of shoes is paved with slate and Mexican river stones.

In the same house, massive spanning logs of pine and fir contrast with the delicate, linear patterns of the walls. The curved beam with the forest fire scar is incense cedar. The reading alcove is a variation on the veranda raised to bench height and open to the outside.

Fine craftsmanship finds its way into every room. Walls are lime plaster, a traditional, formal style.

The classic soaking tub is allowed to stand alone, unadorned and inviting on a tile floor.

The master bedroom is
essentially Japanese
except for the bed whose
height dictated the level
of the windows.

Below: In Hawaii, another East Wind home demonstrates how warm woods, expertly interlocked, preclude additional decor. Western red cedar boards are teamed with Port Orford cedar beams, purlins, posts, *shoji* and doors.

Left above: Entry doors and windows are also Port Orford, which is especially resistant to Hawaii's fierce termites. Bamboo and a local vine form window grating.

Left below: Living room, seen through the *tatami* guest room, has floors of Pennsylvania black cherry which Brackett rates the world's best.

Finely detailed lattice of "wine" redwood
lets island breezes blow through interior.
The wood came from 90-year-old casks
from a California vineyard.

Port Orford cedar and ponderosa pine
meet in a classic scarf joint. Jalousies
are concealed from sight, inside and
out, between two sets of gratings.

Joan and Jerry Rolnick are full of surprises. One day a friend at the United Nations asked them to entertain two visitors from Japan at their Connecticut home. The guests looked around at the authentic Japanese-style quarters, exclaimed with delight, and then asked, "But where do you live?" They thought they were visiting a museum. They couldn't believe that an American couple with four children would choose to live so minimally.

Had the visitors been told the story behind the thatched roof, they would have been even more astounded. Twenty years ago, when Jerry and two of their children built the house with their own hands, Jerry decided that the garage should have a thatch roof. He drove to Long Island Sound to fill his pick-up truck with fragmite reeds. It took 35 truck loads and a large dose of Jerry's overriding philosophy: "Never lose the teen-age attitude that you can do it and that you are invincible." Joan concurs and says, "We have fun together."

Retired now after multiple careers that started as a rodeo rider in his native Texas and progressed through manufacturing, construction, business administration, college administration and finally — after two Masters degrees — a practice in psychotherapy in partnership with his wife, Rolnick still doesn't have enough hours in the day.

On the drawing boards is a teahouse that will rise in a clearing, deep in the woods. But first, he and daughter Kyle have to resolve how to bridge the small valley that separates the site from the house. The property borders four miles of hiking trails, and "you can go for two-and-a-half hours and not see the road," Jerry beams.

Rolnick's whole-hearted admiration for Japanese style stems from frequent business trips to Japan after World War II. A Marine during the war, Rolnick got close to Japan but never managed to get ashore. Not one to hold a grudge, he adds that many Japanese became his best friends and customers in peacetime. He admires the country's culture because "its people are the only ones in the world to make a religion out of aesthetics."

The Rolnick house was born of practicality and incredible tenacity. Jerry and Joan set out in 1972 to buy a smaller house, but everything affordable

Right: Cedar posts have been fashioned into a gate that stands on *Odayaka Roji* (Tranquility Lane).

Japanese river stones make a glistening entry floor. Joan's ingenious fence screens house from the road.

Riding on a sea of pachysandra, one family's version of a Japanese house is inspiration to all who pursue a goal.

Hardy impatiens soften New England boulders in this multi-level backyard, while a patient Buddha overlooks the proposed site for a teahouse.

needed remodeling. Jerry decided if he built his own, he could have his druthers — a Japanese house. He found two illustrated manuals for carpenters written in Japanese, and unfazed, managed to teach himself enough of the language to figure them out.

The Rolnicks' efforts did not stop with completion of the house. They transformed the rocky land as well, doing most of the stonework themselves. Joan flanked their front path with day lilies transplanted from the roadside, and Jerry coaxed the moss from the woods to coat their backyard with velvet. Joan built her own version of a Japanese fence by bracing branches between two horizontal half-round lengths of wood. She replenishes it regularly with sticks gathered on long walks.

In the ultimate do-it-yourself task, the Rolnicks have just completed recovering their 20-year-old *tatami* mats. Even in Japan, this is a job for specialized craftsmen; it took a year to do all 37 of them.

The family's ties to Japan are not relegated to aesthetics alone. They have been continuously renewed through hosting young Japanese students studying at a nearby college. The students, in turn, are eager to reciprocate on the Rolnicks' visits to the Far East. Incurable travelers still, this youthful senior couple set out with weekend bags the day after these photos were taken for a five-week study tour of New Guinea, Borneo and Bali.

The Rolnicks' strongest link to Japan, however, has been forged by their youngest son, Brian. As a rebellious teen-ager, he refused to have any part in the construction of the house. Yet when he was older and perhaps unconsciously converted to things Japanese, he enlisted in the Navy and was assigned to his first choice of posts: Japan. After a few years there, to his parents' delight, he chose a Japanese bride. The ultimate arrival of granddaughter Shino brought more joy to both East and West.

The nine-room house and garden have
brought the resourceful Rolnick family 20
years of pleasure. The backyard gives
way to a forest preserve.

Above: A small decorative balcony, made of "ripped" pressure-treated wood, enhances the view from an upstairs bedroom. The quilted wall hanging is Joan's design.

Right: Guided only by two small manuals in Japanese, Jerry Rolnick designed and built the house following traditional post and beam construction techniques. Japanese bamboo blinds separate the living room from the family room.

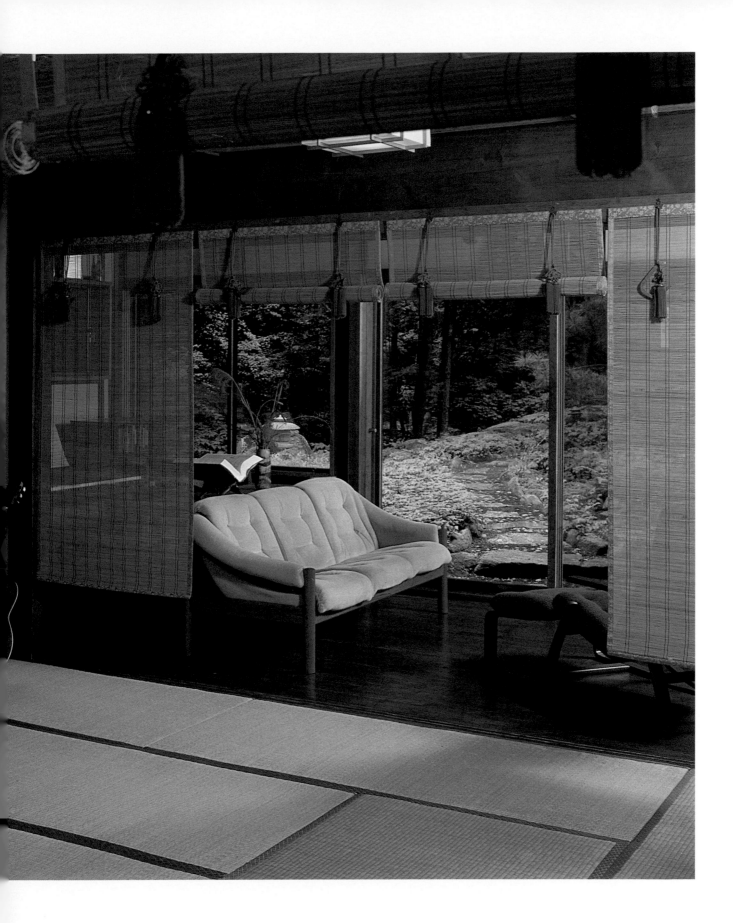

If it is true that a house should be lived in before being remodeled, Faith and Lester Lieberman have been very conservative. They owned their weekend house for 15 years before they threw caution to the East wind, gutted the structure and more than doubled its size for a 7,000-square-foot salute to Japanese design.

Faith Lieberman, the vital force in the renovation, has never been to Japan, but says, "If I were mystical, I would say that in some other life I must have been there." Faith is a designer and sculptor who works in clay and stone, creating moderately large pieces. Nothing she has done, however, equals the time and effort she has expended in reshaping the 40-year-old house in the Japanese spirit.

Built on a high bank overlooking a Long Island, New York harbor, the site is favored with a southern exposure on terraced land that slips away to the water. Tall tree trunks frame portions of the view from every room and every angle. Knowing that the panorama was endlessly appealing to the whole family, the Liebermans had their architect replace the entire front facade with glass to fill the house with light and beauty. Almost all the rooms, including the bedrooms, now open onto generous decks, some edged with protective panels of safety glass below the railing.

"The house was an uninteresting brick ranch," Lester Lieberman explains, "that became more unsatisfying each year." Its new persona evolved from the couple's interest in Japanese antiques and artifacts. As their collection grew, and fine Japanese screens became a key element in their city apartment, they found themselves more and more drawn to the understated, subdued aesthetic of Japanese design and its emphasis on nature as a route to inner serenity. They also realized that many of their Japanese objects were best displayed against the light and simple backgrounds of Japanese style. The fact that this style precludes curtains and drapes, which the Liebermans find intrusive, was another bonus. The couple had discovered the practicality of *shoji* screens earlier when Faith used them extensively in the renovation of her husband's medical offices.

In the classic tradition of Japanese architecture, the new roof of the Lieberman house with its imported Japanese tile is the most memorable feature of

Right: A 40-year-old home, remodeled and doubled in size in 1993, has a discreet front entrance in keeping with Japanese tradition. A *kura* (storehouse) door has been mounted on the end wall, and an ilex has been trimmed to its Japanese soul.

Once a small brick ranch-style house, this expanded 15-room home, overlooking a harbor, begins a new era clad in cypress siding and Weather Shield doors and windows.

Basswood and fiberglass brighten and soften an interior passageway. Windowed *shoji* slides right to frame niche.

Right: In the foyer, a 19th-century cedar horse from a temple surveys the mahogony staircase and wall decorated with cypress doors.

the exterior. The heavy tiles were applied by Japanese roofers who first had to reinforce the substructure. The unusual green color was chosen to blend in with the site's heavily planted slope. Some Japanese roofs are blue, but grey is most common, aging to look like old silver or lead. The green tiles, along with the coral-colored stucco, chosen by the owners for its sunshine quality, are set off by copper-coated aluminum rain gutters and downspouts. "I wanted the gutters to be like a piece of jewelry, like a necklace that lifts the eye," Faith explained.

Inside, raised ceilings soar over a medley of woods for flooring and trim. A mahogany staircase wall in the foyer is recessed in one portion to hold decorative antique Japanese doors. Other antique doors are mounted into actual doors that slide from concealed pockets when privacy is needed in the free-flowing interior. Throughout the house, *shoji* screens in several variations reveal the expertise of Hisao Hanafusa's company, Miya Shoji Interiors. The 15 rooms that Faith designed, all imbued with Japanese simplicity, include such luxuries as a mirrored indoor lap pool and a two-story sculpture studio.

The main room's raised floor, reminiscent of a *tatami* platform, is cherry, contrasting with light maple flooring elsewhere. The focal point of a Japanese interior is generally the sunken firepit for cooking. The Liebermans borrow the concept, but change the function, making it a recessed seating area instead. This one, which even camouflages a TV, is bordered by a hearth and low sofa table, both covered with small tiles that resemble river stones.

Faith did not intend to become the project's general contractor, but she realized that that was the only way to achieve their goals. "Creativity without practicality is foolish," she says. "I realized I had to be on the scene during much of the work to insure that certain ideas would work. If a concept doesn't work, you have to be adaptable. You have to make the most of your mistakes without redoing everything. That's one of the reasons I love asymmetry. It can save you when there's a technical error."

While a large antique wooden horse overlooking the foyer is the home's most striking artifact, the house attracted an even more genuine mascot during reconstruction. A huge, sleepy dog, an Akita who lived in the neighborhood, trotted in each morning at the workmens' heels and snoozed all day in the sunlight, dreaming, no doubt, of his ancestral home, Japan.

Above and right: Century-old reed and bamboo doors mounted in basswood contrast with custom-made table and chairs of cherry in kitchen corner.

Left: A mini-*tatami* area, edged with Western seating, makes a snug nest by the fireplace. Antique teakettle and sculpted hearth hook are suspended above a modern electric burner built into table for entertaining.

Shoji-inspired
windows amplify
the geometrics
the master bath.

Japanese tiles in an unusual green blend with the landscape.

View from master bedroom includes doors with a variation on the *shoji* grid and pau lope decking.

The hallmark of a
Japanese house is found
in well-crafted details.

Climaxing a terraced hill,
the cypress and stucco
garage adds
beauty to function.

Using a flat back lawn as their canvas, a California couple turned their property into a living painting that illuminates all the principal rooms of their elegantly furnished home, which had only faint Japanese architectural styling when they started.

Their goal was privacy, scenery and an appropriate setting for some exceptional garden ornaments. Their triumph is a classic hill-and-pond garden that suggests far greater dimensions than its actual 40- by 80-foot dimensions.

Although the garden was adapted to its site and climate, it was directly inspired by a visit to the famous moss garden at the Saiho-ji Temple in Kyoto. The owner showed a picture of it to his landscaper, the late Nagao Sakurai, at their first meeting for assurance that the moss in the new garden would be similar. Undaunted, Sakurai pointed out that the Kyoto garden was 600 years old, but promised that if the owner could wait 600 years, his would look just the same.

Sakurai started with the first essential component, a fence. Enclosure of space is indispensable in Japanese gardens in order to define relationships. More than a demarcation, a fence also psychologically separates domestic space from the outside world. But a fence draws a firm, unequivocal line, so Sakurai also planted a hedge inside the fence to blur boundaries. Rather than using one species that would be trimmed uniformly, he planted a mix of bushes, resulting in varying color, texture and height to further the illusion of depth. He made sure that three tall trees in a neighboring yard were incorporated into the view, "borrowing scenery" as the Japanese say, to create more expansiveness.

He then brought in truckloads of top soil to exaggerate a slight upward slope of the land, which he planted heavily to suggest a hilly, forested terrain. The "mountain" became the apparent origin of the garden's most dynamic feature: a stream that flows on the diagonal across two-thirds of the plot and broadens into a small pond, allowing a gentle waterfall to add its melody to the rustle of the trees. And to protect the resident carp which kept falling prey to uninvited raccoons, the owners hid a metal grid under the water lilies at one end of the pond where the fish could dart to safety.

In general, hill-and-pond gardens are not designed for strolling, but are created to provide serene views from several perspectives. To increase the sense

A small courtyard garden sets the theme in the foyer. The bamboo fence mounted on the siding makes a discreet but powerful contribution.

of unity, restraint and rhythm, a limited but harmonious range of species was used repeatedly. Pruning trees severely keeps them on a human scale and in proportion to other components. They are shaped to reveal each species' essential nature.

The owners continued the Japanese theme into a tab of land (20 by 24 feet) that divides both wings of the four-bedroom house and begins at a glass-walled foyer. This courtyard garden, which opens onto the main garden, immediately sets the theme as the front door opens. Drainage pipes concealed at the base of the building dictated a stony border, which has been ingeniously

Right: A stream, whose source is purposely concealed, widens into a pond. A pair of cranes, symbols of longevity, stand near the carp, symbols of perseverance.

Far right: The pond is fed by a waterfall designed to evoke the spirit of a dense woodland.

incorporated into the overall design. In order to link the land and the house thematically, small but significant adjustments to the house make a smooth transition from structure to garden. *Shoji* screens frame the views from within and one exterior wall has been faced with a bamboo fence.

The unrivaled stars of the scene, however, are its antique ornaments, a stone pagoda and a lantern from California's 1915 Panama Pacific Exposition and two enormous ceramic jardinieres, dating from 6th century China, which give the garden, now 30 years old, a direct tie to its Asian roots.

Right and below: A regal lantern is reflected in the tranquil pond.

A natural bridge, anchored on stones in the traditional manner, leads to a small island.

Various species of moss, including jewel mint of Corsica and baby's tears, unify the plantings and accentuate the historic lantern.

Karl and Pearl Meissner gazed at the sloping, wind-swept land studded with forbidding boulders and declared it perfect. They had spent two years, starting in 1952, hunting for a building site with a commanding view of the Hudson River where they could create their personal vision of a Japanese home.

Their search had intensified after a casual visit to New York's Museum of Modern Art when they lost their hearts to an import. On exhibit in the museum's garden was a full-sized Japanese house that had been shipped from Nagoya in 700 crates and reassembled, complete with fences, furnishings and stones. The Meissners were drawn to the peacefulness of the house and the close relation of its indoor and outdoor areas. Karl was impressed by its craftsmanship, especially its use of wood. Gazing at the reconstruction in the museum, he resolved to make his own Japanese house — with his own hands. Once the Hudson River site was

bought, he drew up plans and began to build, working weekends and nights after his regular business day. Two years later, the Meissners moved in and 13 years later, Karl pronounced the house finished.

Meissner was no stranger to design. In 1917, as a 15-year-old, skilled (but poorly paid) map draftsman, he changed careers and became an ornamental plasterer like his father. Until the 1929 Depression, he added aesthetic touches to many of Manhattan's important buildings, including the Waldorf Astoria. When construction work grew scarce during the lean years of the 1930's, Meissner, a fine artist by avocation, turned to sign painting and eventually took up silkscreen printing. He patented the country's first automatic silkscreen printing machine and went on to develop his own prosperous business on Manhattan's Lower East Side.

Karl's wife, Pearl, explains that she was drawn to Far Eastern themes even as a child. In her hometown of Boulder, Colorado, she met visiting missionaries from the Orient. "I loved hearing their tales of life in China and Japan," she recalled, "and was fascinated by the photographs they brought back." Eventually, her career brought her to Brooklyn College to teach psychology and, ultimately, to meet and marry Karl.

Patterned partly after a masterpiece of
Japanese domestic architecture, this American
version stays as ageless as its
cascading garden.

Although Pearl was very much involved with every step of the project, she feels that "The house is testimony to one man's perseverance and resourcefulness, since Karl became a self-taught expert, searching out books to learn the essentials of Japanese design, joinery and landscaping."

The couple explain that their four-bedroom home is saddled on a rise over a few of the boulders, the best spot on the property to see the river and enjoy the cascading garden. Part of its design, Karl points out, is a copy of the museum house. It even has an interior carp pond like the original, which divides the living area from the dining room. The pond, surrounded by tropical plants, is reminiscent of a naturally landscaped pool with a small waterfall. The area seems to be an extension of the outside garden from which it is separated by eight-foot windows, a Western element that Karl added.

Another Western feature was the use of native woods for the project: Florida cypress, California redwood, oak from the local lumber yard and birch from the Meissners' land. The stuccowork was Karl's bailiwick, of course, but he also did the stonework, inside and out, the ornamental woodwork, and most of the *shoji*, which demand meticulous carpentry. These wood and paper screens added an important weather barrier before the advent of double glazed glass. Later, the construction of additional *shoji* was turned over to professionals.

Finally, Karl and Pearl completed their dream by transforming the rocky terrain with a carefully planned Japanese garden, one which they maintained themselves for 36 years. Now at the age of 86, Pearl has reluctantly stopped the outside work, turning over its care to a gardener — not because of age — but because of recurring Lyme Disease.

In 1983 and again in 1985, the Meissners achieved another aspect of their dream. They returned to Japan where they had visited briefly decades before. This time they focused on design, taking in more than they could assimilate in their short weeks there. And they made three timeless purchases: three stone lanterns came home with them to join the rocks of the Palisades in a final East-West alliance.

Right above: Honeysuckle and brambles occupied the rocky site when the land was acquired. Slowly, a Japanese garden took root and, with constant attention and drastic pruning through four decades, has provided continual delight.

Right below: The front entrance welcomes visitors with a varied display of plantings. Hardy bamboo flanks the slate steps and survives a northern exposure.

The master bedroom opens
onto a corner deck looking
toward the river.

A winding stroll down
through the garden leads to
unexpected sights, such as
this weeping cherry tree.

The backyard is bordered by a stand of giant bamboo where wild deer take refuge.

Under a sheltering roof, the wraparound deck allows communion with nature through the four seasons.

Art designers view space as a medium. Their goal is to maximize it, which can sometimes mean not filling it. Or, in the case of Swiss designer Erich Aeschlima, transforming it into movable space that serves three functions at once.

When Aeschlima and his wife, Eva, acquired 2,000 sq. feet of empty loft in Manhattan's SoHo district, Erich eagerly accepted the challenge of arranging it. First, he converted the front third into sleek living quarters with tile floors, black leather and glass furnishings plus a gleaming white kitchen. The rest of the space was to house the bedroom, Erich's studio, and occasionally, an art gallery.

But having gone high tech with the living quarters and having concealed all the time-worn features of the 100-year-old building, the Aeschlimas became more protective of the rich oak floor that remained. Erich's initial impulse was to create a granite-like box for a master bedroom that would rest on the floor but not coordinate with it. "Too austere," he decided. Next, he briefly considered a glossy black, Italianate cube that would echo the spirit of the front quarters. "Too repetitive," he concluded.

Then his thoughts turned to Japanese chests and teahouses. A Japanese design would satisfy his need for linear purity, while beautifully crafted wood would accord with the long expanse of floor. And, it occurred to him, if he created a Japanese bedroom on concealed wheels, he would be left with very flexible space for his own design work or exhibitions. The bedroom could be repositioned according to the needs of the day.

Aeschlima's "space within a space" serves sleeping, storage and decorative functions simultaneously. In the Japanese tradition, he has created flexible rather than specific space. "I'm not really a Japanophile," Aeschlima says, "although I greatly respect their use of wood and their fidelity to traditional craft techniques. But I know it's impossible to be really Japanese no matter how long you try. I've been in this country so long, I feel 80 percent American, which," he adds with a grin, "is just about as American as everyone else."

Right: A movable bedroom allows a Manhattan loft to be mostly an art studio. Concealed wheels make it easy to push the cube out of the way.

New York being New York, Aeschlima did not have far to look for qualified carpenters to execute his concept. Tansuya, a neighborhood Japanese construction company specializing in chests and interiors, built the 10- by 10-foot cube to his specifications. Aeschlima's research of Japanese design led him to the favorite book of many designers represented in this volume: Edward S. Morse's classic, *Japanese Homes and Their Surroundings,* first published in 1886. Morse took special delight in figuring out how things are put together, as does Aeschlima, schooled in industrial design and architecture in Switzerland. He sees his company, Aeschlima Design, as a studio whose first work is "creative problem-solving" by putting things together in new ways.

The teahouse-turned-bedroom is one of these new ways with its proportions, Erich points out, not precisely traditional. Its dimensions were determined to accommodate the queen-sized mattress (60 by 80 inches).

A custom-made *tansu* or storage chest on the exterior wall was lifted into its niche for a built-in look. The hardware on the drawers was harder to come by until a blacksmith in Switzerland agreed to forge them from a drawing.

The cocoon-like sleeping arrangements are very soothing, the couple says, and the *shoji* walls provide extra insulation from city noise. The cube's mobility also allows it to be positioned to catch extra breezes or more heat, while the moon window, a distinctive aesthetic device in Japanese architecture, provides additional ventilation. In a Japanese room, the post in the display alcove is the most important piece of wood, as it is here: a piece of cypress found at the beach.

"In a sense, my cube represents the concept of inside-outside space of Japan. My outside space is American. First, we come into this 1880 building, then at the top of the stairs into 1990-style space, and then into Japanese space. When Eva goes out to her travel agency in the morning, she has already traveled through three eras before she reaches the sidewalk."

"When you think about it," Aeschlima says, "this mix is what New York is all about. It's a fascinating city because it never allows you to be confined to your culture. You can't think that your type of bread is the right bread for everyone or your thought the only right thought."

The large portraits are by New York painter/illustrator Linda Fennimore.

A custom-made storage chest of solid cherry fits snugly into the teahouse which is framed with fir and faced with painted plywood, chosen for its lightweight.

Traveling in Japan, Barbara Wilson came across advice from an ancient sage: "Enjoy the land, but don't harm it. Preserve its beauty for your descendants."

This counsel took root and years later became Barbara's guiding principle in building a small home on inherited land in California. Her retreat on the dramatic Point Reyes seacoast hugs a wooded hill, taking shelter under tall branches. Disturbing the forest as little as possible, it is built in the Japanese spirit to allow relaxation with nature. It also provides a quiet climax to Barbara's daily commute from San Francisco through the billowing green and straw hills of Marin County.

Yet, just as important to Barbara, the house also delights visiting grandchildren. Cozy sleeping alcoves and lofts, fragrant with straw mats, invite repose and shared confidences. Barbara created two separate living areas on two floors, using the lower floor (and only 975 sq. feet) for herself. Apart from her bedroom, the rest of her living space is essentially one room. Now that the children are gone, she explains, this space is large enough for her, yet flexible enough to accommodate large family reunions. Barbara turned the upper living space into an area for guests. Japanese visitors, in particular, are happy to find familiar furnishings in their quarters and may unwind, for example, at a *kotatsu*, a low openwork table draped with a quilt. The heater underneath warms the lower body and makes sitting on the floor a cozy, shared experience.

In San Francisco, Barbara works in a Japanese antiques showroom. Her love of things Japanese is an outgrowth of her passion for *bonsai* which she taught for many years. When she began looking for an architect five years ago, she wanted one who not only shared her respect for nature, she also needed a collaborator on the design of a *bonsai* work area near the new house.

Paul Korhummel of Marin County endorsed her goals and developed her ideas "beyond expectations." Tall trees were incorporated into the plans rather than felled, and several features of Japanese traditional architecture were used to bring the outside in. Because the site's location is a few miles from the epicenter of the 1906 earthquake, the structure rests on 15-foot pilings. An overall Japanese feeling was achieved partly by using the country's 3- by 6-foot design

Right: A forest retreat encourages the woods to come close to the house. The low veranda anchors the house to the land. An antique Japanese *hibachi* or brazier holds the *bonsai*.

Left: A 20-year-old Corkbark elm, a Japanese maple grove, and a 60-year-old *hinoki* cypress catch the sun in a protected corner of the potting shed's enclosure.

Right: California redwood combines with zelkova doors brought from Japan. Inside, this potting shed is more homey than scruffy. The antique *kanji* signboard says "School of Tea Ceremony and Flower Arranging."

unit for the building's proportions. Even the baths are influenced by Japan: their American stall showers double as soaking tubs — thanks to a 30-inch recession below the floor. As for the *bonsai* potting shed, it stands a few steps from the front door and, with its compact loft, resembles a miniature house.

Inside the main house, the mellow tones of bamboo shades, reed screens, *shoji* and selected Japanese antiques combine readily with a few pieces of Victorian furniture, handed down like the land. Local redwood used in construction accords with sand carpeting and grasscloth.

"At this point in my life, I like old things, not the new and shiny. I don't want to have to worry about possessions. I want comfortable, old things." Barbara's own chair for relaxing is a straight-backed upholstered heirloom set against an interior wall, a strategic spot to watch the sunlight shimmer through the woods. "I don't care for grass," Barbara confesses, so she has encouraged the woods to return to the edge of her narrow porch by planting native California plants. Close to the ground and shaded by a 4-foot roof overhang, the 42-foot long porch was inspired by the *engawa* that connects the traditional Japanese house to the land.

Although grass doesn't appeal to Barbara, she has always loved gardening. "When I was first married, I moved too often and had to leave whole gardens behind. I took up *bonsai* in order to take my garden with me, and it was *bonsai* that introduced me to the arts of Japan, since I needed screens and scrolls to serve as appropriate backdrops." Now the subject matter of those screens and scrolls — nature at its most graceful — is the backdrop of her daily life.

A guest room with a difference. Step out to a second floor aerie to see the forest, full-size or miniature. Or step up to a *tatami* nook for a peaceful night on a *futon*. Antique reed sliding doors form the alcove's wall.

While most of the homeowners represented in this book became well-versed in Japanese architecture during the process of construction, two other families, uninitiated to things Japanese, were spontaneously converted by already completed homes.

These vintage houses, one in the horse country of suburban New York, and the other on the famous 17-Mile Drive along the California coast, were for sale when they made their conquests.

The New York house had been built on a wooded lane in 1955 by an artist/sculptor who wanted a home that would absorb the drama of the seasons and the daily changes of light on the beautiful rolling terrain. She commis-

In winter or summer the structures embrace the landscape.

sioned the late Philip Ives to design a house that would have a strong Japanese influence and generous views of the property. A year after its completion, the house had become so inviting that Ives was asked to add guest quarters. Instead of expanding the house, Ives positioned a small Japanese cottage a few yards away and connected it to the main house by an indirect covered walkway. The Japanese favor indirect routes for a number of reasons. In ancient days, a circuitous route confounded palace attackers, a fact which no doubt gave rise to the superstition that "evil follows straight lines." On a more aesthetic level, an indirect route is more graceful and since it affords many more views of the landscape than a straight one, it is a cherished device of classical Japanese gardeners. Situated slightly downhill from the main house, the detached guest house permits enjoyment of a different part of the terrain.

When the award-winning house went up for resale in 1971, a Manhattan family bought it without hesitation and decided to add a pool and a poolhouse to make it their ideal, year-round escape from city life. Philip Ives was again invited to provide his interpretation of Japanese architecture. For his design, Ives drew inspiration from the Shishinden, the imperial palace in Kyoto, modeling the poolhouse after a section of the gallery that overlooks the palace's famous sand garden. While the Shishinden is used only on ceremonial occasions, its American counterpart shelters leisure time activities.

With its dark frame seeming to repeat the lines of the towering trees on the rolling grounds, the poolhouse provides a third vantage point for enjoyment of the varied landscape: tended lawns enlivened by dramatic boulders, historic fieldstone walls, friendly wildlife and a picturesque wooded valley backed by low hills. Far from intruding on the scene, the structures embrace the landscape, becoming an amphitheater for its unrivaled show.

Drawing inspiration from an imperial building in Kyoto, the poolhouse offers generous shade and the added convenience of a small kitchen. Japanese touches accent the grounds.

A covered, indirect walkway, typically Japanese, leads to the guest house, whose design demonstrates that the most expressive feature of Japanese architecture is the roof. It's a short walk to the poolhouse, pictured at the top, which complements the buildings.

PACIFIC OUTLOOK

On the opposite coast, the other house, *Tengoku* (Heavenly Abode) stands on a bluff overlooking the Pacific Ocean. Although it also overlooks a busy stretch of the famed 17-Mile Drive around the Monterey Peninsula, a California couple looking for a retirement home 20 years ago were immediately captivated. They bought the Japanese-inspired, redwood contemporary when it was 12 years old.

Designed by Carmel architect Walter Burde to appear to rise out of the rocks, *Tengoku* looks out over the Pacific Ocean. The roof ornament, a fish which is a symbol in Japan of good luck and protection against fires, turns seaward.

Knowing nothing of its background, the second owners thought it well-named since it was so peaceful. Later they came to meet the architect, Walter Burde FAIA, who described his challenge in designing it. The original owners had lived in the Far East and wanted a harmonious setting for their collection of Japanese furnishings. Since the property was filled with huge boulders that couldn't be moved, Burde took his sketch pad to the property, and measuring distances between the rocks, designed it on the site. Burde's work over a 57-year career included many homes in a Japanese style, as well as the Buddhist Temple in nearby Seaside, but none of the other residences, he says, were as large or as challenging as *Tengoku.*

The second owners still take great pleasure in its restful personality and enjoy the many additional moods provided by the sea. When the fog drifts in, misting the sloping garden and enveloping the house, the location evokes the hillside settings of Japanese silk screens. The throngs of tourists are no problem. Clustered across the street, they invariably look out to sea and miss the house partially hidden behind a handsome wooden fence, like a lovely Japanese woman waiting demurely behind a fan.

Only the eastern facade suggests the size of the four-bedroom house. In general, Japanese houses are not designed to look imposing from the street. One must slowly discover a building's layout.

"To me, the real spirit of Japanese architecture is its never-ending sense of nature. Not just in terms of vistas, but in feeling the *spirit* of wood, feeling the spirit of adobe, feeling the spirit of the sun's energy," says Travis Price, an award-winning architect. Price is passionate about his subject in the gently persuasive way of his native South. "'Less is more' was really a bad thing for America," he continues. "It drained things to a utilitarian sterility. I like to think of what I do as 'minimalism with a soul.'"

Although Price's work, with one exception, is not a literal rendering of Japanese architecture, he uses imaginative ways to embrace its philosophical core, making the inside and outside one. At the same time, he draws on sophisticated technologies to make all his structures energy efficient.

One client, whose ample estate in Washington, D.C. included a swimming pool, enjoyed the way the water reflected a large grove of bamboo. The pleasant vignette gave her an idea: since she needed a place to sketch, why not create a small Japanese pavilion at the water's edge and extend the reflecting pool concept? Price's design, which bridged two existing cabanas, gave her not only a studio, but also additional guest quarters and a meditative retreat in the philosophical spirit of the classic teahouse. In old Japan, no matter how lavish the main house became, homeowners wanting to stay attuned to the cosmos retreated to a humble teahouse on the property to maintain mental balance. Price's version, only 600 square feet, has become the client's most important space, allowing respite from a busy lifestyle. She says, "Of all my homes, this is where I feel most comfortable, most centered."

At night, the pavilion looks like a giant *shoji* lamp with walls of four-inch translucent, insulated fiberglass, called Kalwalls. The product consists of two large sheets of fiberglass with a core of clear insulating fibers that transmits up to 80 percent of natural light, considerably more than conventional *shoji.* Virtually indestructible, the panels become Japanese with the imposition of metal grids.

The structure's frame, made of fragrant Port Orford cedar milled on the West Coast, is capped by a lead-coated stainless steel roof, "the best of the best," Price points out. A teak rib gives a Japanese fillip to the peak. Decks of

Right: A wooden path leads through bamboo to a painting studio, whose small space, like the teahouse of old Japan, is calculated to promote wabi, *"calm simplicity."*

Alaskan cedar have been cantilevered over the water to tie the pavilion to the pool. Even the original bamboo grove has been improved upon. Mirrors have been placed at both ends to allow a study of self and bamboo into infinity.

Price, a native of Georgia, spent the early part of his professional life in the Southwest designing large solar housing complexes and the world's largest solar construction, a one-million-square-foot building for the Tennessee Valley Authority. In 1979, he came back East to Takoma Park, Maryland, to add other dimensions to his work and to teach in his leisure time at various universities. He is currently guiding graduate architecture students at Catholic University.

Price puts into his buildings three main elements that he calls "sunshine, temples and highways." Of the first element, he says, "I like to remember what a sunrise means to me." Therefore, he designs homes which not only fill with natural light, but also open readily and totally to the fresh air. The second element, the temple quality, is the home's ability to provide "quiet time," a peaceful interlude for looking within. He says that the third element, the highway, is almost inherent in the definition of American. It is his metaphor for big, sweeping curves, an expansiveness that must be retained in American design. More succinctly, he wants a sense of timeliness (nature), timelessness (temples) and timefulness (highways) "colliding harmoniously."

Occupying a corner of a Washington, D.C. estate, the painting studio displays its luminous, insulated, indestructible *shoji* walls.

Of all Travis Price's "sunrise, temples and highway" work, John and Patricia Carleton's Maryland home is the most dramatic. Springing from the Carletons' interest in Asian architecture, its design meets the couple's need for a home that is minimalist yet ethereal. Price sees it as a "never-ending garden path." The front door opens to a flood of sunlight and views that take you outdoors again. "You never stop — and yet, you are always still," he says.

John Carleton wanted to include a carp pond on the property, so Price added it to the deck, making it almost part of the interior. The architect decided to include four of the five essential elements in ancient Japanese cosmology: fire and earth in the black granite fireplace, water in the pond at its perimeter and air in the vaulted rooms .

Another design direction was to make the structure appear to float, thus achieving the desired ethereal quality that is the goal in Zen meditation: you are floating in your body, your body is floating in the universe. The curved lines (highways) of the interior railings plus the stepped decks outside which repeat the steps of the Japanese garden, all contribute to the floating feeling. As Price points out, "The house is a meditative moment of structural elements — roof floating above you, landscape flowing underneath you."

Decompression back to nature begins in the driveway, which is tufted with grass, the result of paving it with interlocking concrete blocks called "Grasscrete." Driving across them produces a delicate clinking sound, a doorbell in effect, but to Price, it is akin to the nightingale boards in the *samurai* houses where floorboards were left loose to announce the approach of an attacker. Price designed the 7,000-square-foot house to use as little energy as possible in spite of the wide climactic range of the region. Its glassed

A Maryland home blends a Japanese soul with energy-saving efficiency.

A gentle pond with flitting carp, an age-old outlet for relaxation, borders the living room. A stepped chimney repeats the lines of the house.

A lap pool, with bleached cedar planking, serves as exercise space, a solar heat sink, a meditative sight and an ideal display area for John Carleton's carefully tended *bonsai.*

southern facade pulls in the sun, yet tall trees shade it in summer. The other timber-framed walls hold three times the normal amount of insulation and are coated with an acrylic stucco chosen for its energy-saving qualities. It's a naturally smart house, says Price, where the temperature remains at 70 degrees without using excessive amounts of fossil fuels or complex technologies. "The building opens its envelope to the sun," Price continues "and works with nature in a much stronger way than the traditional Japanese house." All of the glass opens, so the house can be quickly cross-ventilated. The enclosed lap pool off the living room doubles as a heat sink for passive solar heating. In winter, opening the doors to the living room allow its heat and humidity to permeate the rest of the house. In summer, its glass walls can be opened for an outdoor experience. All year long, the pool is both an exercise area and a meditative one, offering the interior a soothing view.

Outdoors, generous woods bound the property. The Carletons' reverence for nature has been so heightened by their new home that, like the families of ancient Japan, the only art within their house comes from the outside, the living images of nature.

Its southern facade cut
away, the sculptural, yet
ethereal home reaches out
to the light and the land.

Page 14: Naga Antiques, 145 E. 61st Street, New York, NY 10021. Tel. (212) 593-2788.

Page 26: David H. Engel, Landgarden Landscape Architects, 215 Park Avenue South, New York, NY 10003. Tel. (212) 228-9500. Stone stream by John DeRiu Masonry Corp., 39 Joy Road, Middlebury, CT 06762. Tel. (203) 758-9794.

Page 40: Chadine Flood Gong, Chadine Interior Design, 15910 Ravine Road, Los Gatos, CA 95030. Tel. (408) 354-0606.

Page 50: Antiques from Dandelion, 2877 California Street, San Francisco, CA 94115. Tel. (415) 563-3100, and Tampopo, 410 Townsend Street, Space 400, San Francisco, CA 94107. Tel. (415) 979-0456.

Page 60: Len Brackett, East Wind Inc., 21020 Shields Camp Road, Nevada City, CA 93959. Tel. (916) 265-3744. Price Crozer Designs, 512 Wilson Avenue, Novato, CA 94947. Tel. (415) 898-4324. Bill Eichenberger Custom Woodwork, 580 Irwin #6, San Rafael, CA 94901. Tel. (415) 457-1190. Jerri Golden Interiors, 2518 Union, San Francisco, CA 94123. Tel. (415) 346-2660. Zachary Klarich Fine Woodworking, 1447 Stevenson Street, San Francisco, CA 94103. Tel. (415) 621-2066. Donald Keith Olsen Associates AIA, 666 Bridegway, Sausalito, CA 94965. Tel. (415) 332-0297. Sanders Pitman, Marc Miyasato Design, 1355 Donner Avenue, San Francisco, CA 94124. Tel. (415) 822-5854. Antiques from Imari Inc., 40 Filbert Avenue, Sausalito, CA 94965. Tel. (415) 332-0245, Fax (415) 332-3621.

Page 68: Joe Sam Queen, architect, 117 Pigeon Street, Waynesville, NC 28786. Tel. (704) 452-1688. Shoji screens by Miya Shoji Interiors, 109 W. 17th Street, New York, NY 10011. Tel. (212) 243-6774. Five Eggs, formerly in Manhattan, has moved to: Plaza Mercado 212 B, 112 West San Francisco St., Sante Fe NM 87501. Tel. (505) 986-3403.

Page 76: Stephen Morrell, landscape designer, 57 Cedar Lake Road, Chester, CT 06412. Tel. (203) 526-1558.

Page 92: Teahouse constructed by Miya Shoji Interiors. See page 68 above.

Page 98: Garden by Kikuchi Landscape Inc., 1400 Dell Ave., Suite C, Campbell, CA 95008. Mailing address: P.O. Box 110635, Campbell, CA 95011-0635. Tel. (408) 377-8426.

Page 104: Len Brackett, see page 60 above.

Page 128: Screens by Miya Shoji Interiors, see page 68 above. Antiques from Naga Antiques, see page 14 above, and from Vallin Galleries, 516 Danbury Rd., Wilton, CT 06897. Tel. (203) 762-7441. Interior Design by Faith Lieberman, Building Concepts and Design, 400 E. 56th St., New York, NY 10022. Tel. (516) 549-8831. Unusual woods: Monteath Molding, P.O. Box 757, South Amboy, N.J. 08879. Tel. 1-800-922-1029. Roof tiles: International Roofing Products, 1832 South Brand Blvd, #200, Glendale, CA 91204. Tel. (818) 547-6699. "Damtite" synthetic stucco applied by L & M Prochilo, 27 Olesner Dr., Northport, N.Y. 11768 Tel. (516) 757-6047.

Page 152: Aeschlima Design, 307 Fifth Avenue, New York, NY 10016. Tel. (212) 685-1585. Teahouse construction by Tansuya Corp., 159 Mercer Street, New York, NY 10011. Tel. (212) 966-1782.

Page 158: Paul Korhummel Design and Construction, P.O. Box 317, Inverness CA 94937. Tel. (415) 663-9148.

Page 170: Travis Price, Architects, Inc., 7050 Carroll Ave., Takoma Park, Maryland 20912. Tel. (301) 270-9222. Kalwall Corp., Scott Keller, P.O. Box 237, 1111 Candia Road, Manchester, NH 03103. Tel. 800-258-9777.

Bamboo

The American Bamboo Society, comprising 900 members in 35 countries, each year publishes a source list for bamboo plants. Their current list numbers 119 species and specifies 26 dealers in various parts of the U.S., many of whom ship worldwide. To obtain a free copy, send a self-adressed, stamped envelope with your request to The American Bamboo Society, P.O. Box 640, Springville, CA 93265.
Bamboo may also be ordered from Bamboo & Rattan Inc., 470 Oberlin Avenue South, Lakewood, NJ 08701. Tel. (201) 370-0220.

PUBLIC JAPANESE GARDENS

ALABAMA
Birmingham Botanical Gardens
2612 Lane Park Road
Birmingham 35223

Japanese Garden of
Gulf States Paper Corporation
1400 River Road
Tuscaloosa 35401

CALIFORNIA
Hakone Gardens
21000 Big Basin Way
Saratoga 95070

Huntington Botanical Gardens
1151 Oxford Road
San Marino 91108

Japanese Friendship Garden
1490 Senter Road
San Jose 95100

Japanese Tea Garden
Golden Gate Park
San Francisco 94117

Sherman Foundation Library
and Gardens
2647 East Coast Highway
Corona Del Mar 92625

COLORADO
Denver Botanic Gardens
909 York Street
Denver 80206

DISTRICT OF COLUMBIA
Ippakutei, The Ceremonial
Teahouse and Garden at the
Embassy of Japan
2520 Massachusetts Avenue,
N.W. Washington D.C. 20008
(By reservation only)

U.S. National Arboretum
24th and R Streets, N.E.
Washington, DC 20002

FLORIDA
The Morikami Museum and
Japanese Gardens
4000 Morikami Park Road
Delray Beach 33446

San-Ai-An Garden
MacArthur Causeway
Watson Island
Miami 33100

GEORGIA
Atlanta Botanical Garden
Piedmont Road at The Prado
Box 77246
Atlanta 30357

The Jimmy Carter Library
1 Copenhill Avenue
Atlanta 30307

HAWAII
East-West Center
University of Hawaii
Manoa Campus
1777 East-West Road
Honolulu 96822

Honolulu Memorial Park
22 Craigside Place
Honolulu 96817

Kepaniwai Heritage Gardens
Highway 32
Wailuku 96793

Liliuokalani Gardens Park
Banyan Drive and Lihiwai Streets
Hilo 96720

Soto Mission of Hawaii
1708 Nuuanu Avenue
Honolulu 96817

ILLINOIS
Sansho-En
Chicago Botanic Garden
775 Dundee Road
Glencoe 60022

Scovill Gardens Park
71 South Country Club Road
Decatur 62521

LOUISIANA
Live Oak Gardens
Jefferson Island
New Iberia 70560

MARYLAND
Breezewood Japanese Garden
and Museum
3722 Hess Road
Monkton 2111

Brookside Garden
Glenallen Avenue
Wheaton 20902

MASSACHUSETTS
Tenshin-En
Museum of Fine Arts
230 Fenway
Boston 02115

MICHIGAN
Dow Gardens
1018 West Main Street
Midland 48640

Fernwood Botanic Garden
and Nature Center
13988 Range Line Road
Niles 49120

MISSISSIPPI
Mynelle Gardens
4738 Clinton Boulevard
Jackson 39216

MISSOURI
Missouri Botanical Garden
2315 Tower Grove Avenue
St. Louis 63110

NEW JERSEY
Georgian Court College
Lakewood Avenue
Lakewood 08701

NEW YORK
Brooklyn Botanic Garden
1000 Washington Avenue
Brooklyn 11225

The John P. Humes Japanese
Stroll Garden
Dogwood Lane, Mill Neck 11765

OHIO
Garden Center of Greater
Cleveland
11030 East Boulevard
Cleveland 44106

OREGON
Chisen-Kaiyu-Shiki
Japanese Garden
611 SW Kington Street
Portland 97201

PENNSYLVANIA
Japanese House and Gardens
P.O. Box 2224
Fairmount Park Horticultural Cen.
North Horticultural Drive
Philadelphia 19103

Swiss Pine Gardens of Japan
The Arnold Bartschi Foundation
Charleston Road
Malvern 19355

SOUTH CAROLINA
The Japanese Garden
Furman Univesity
3300 Poinsett Highway
Greenville 29613

TENNESSEE
Japanese Tea Garden
Tennessee Botanical Gardens
and Fine Arts Center
Forrest Park Drive
Nashville 37205

Memphis Botanic Garden
750 Cherry Road
Memphis 38117

TEXAS
Japanese Garden
Fort Worth Botanic Garden Cen.
3220 Botanic Garden Drive
Fort Worth 76107

UTAH
International Peace Gardens
10th South and 8th West Streets
Salt Lake City 84109

Japanese Garden
Norfolk Botanical Gardens
Airport Road
Norfolk 23518

WASHINGTON
Japanese Garden
University of Washington
Arboretum
East Madison and Lake
Washington Blvd.
East Seattle 98105

*A list of Japanese gardens in
Europe, Australia, New Zealand
and Canada, plus a more
extensive list of Japanese gar-
dens in the U.S., is available from
The International Association of
Japanese Gardens, Inc.,
One World Trade Center
121 S.W. Salmon Street, Suite 1100,
Portland, Oregon 97204.
Tel: (503) 464-8889 Fax: (503) 464-2299*

*Information on public gardens in
Japan may be obtained by
writing to The Garden Society of
Japan, Mr. Takenosuke Tatsui,
Director, Fukuda Building 301,
6-3, 1-chome, Nishi-Waseda,
Shinjuku-ku, 169 Tokyo.
Tel: Tokyo (03) 3204-0595
Fax: Tokyo (03) 3202-5394*

SPECIALIZED SHOPS

These shops, specializing in antiques and folkcraft, a small sample of hundreds of shops in the country, all have English-speaking sales people and will provide receipts documenting authenticity of antiques.

For antiques:

House of Antiques, 5-15-5 Kajiwara, Kamakura. By appointment only. Tel. (0467) 43-1441/Fax 0467-45-8245.

Fuso Antiques, 1-20-2, Kamata, Ohta-ku, Tokyo 144. Tel. (03) 3730-6530 or 3442-1945. 10 to 6. Closed Sat.& Sun.

Kikori Antique Gallery, 1-9-1, Hibarigaoka, Hoya-shi, Tokyo 202. Tel. (0424) 21-7373. 10 to 6. Retail and wholesale.

Kurochiku Co. Ltd., 34 Takenokaido-cho, Takehana, Yamashina-ku, Kyoto. Tel. (075) 501-8491/Fax 075- 501-8493.

Kurofune, 7-7-4 Roppongi, Minato-ku, Tokyo 106. Tel. 3479-1552. 10 to 6. Closed Sun., holidays.

Magatani Co. Ltd., 5-10-13 Toranomon, Minato-ku, Tokyo 105. Tel. 3433-6321. 10 to 6. Closed Sun. and holidays.

Morita, 5-12-2 Minami Aoyama, Minato-ku, Tokyo107. Tel. 3407-4466. Weekdays 10 to 7, Sun. and holidays 12 to 6.

Nakamura Antiques, 2-24-9 Nishi-azabu, Minato-ku, Tokyo 106. Tel. 3486-0636. 10:30 to 6:30. Closed Tues. Retail and wholesale.

Okura Oriental Art, 3-3-14 Azabudai, Minato-ku, Tokyo 106. Tel. 3585-5309. 10 to 6. Closed Mon.

Osugi Shoten, Gokomachi Sanjo Sagaru, Nakagyo-ku, Kyoto 604. Tel. (075) 231-7554.

For folkcraft:

Bingoya, 10-6 Wakamatsu-cho, Shinjuku-ku, Tokyo 162. Tel. 3202-8778. 10 to 7. Closed Mon.

Oriental Bazaar, 3-9-13 Jingumae, Shibuya-ku, Tokyo 150. Tel. 3400-3933. 9:30 to 6:30. Closed Thurs. Also carries antiques.

Prefecture Showrooms, Daimaru Department Store and Kokusai Kanko Building, next to Tokyo Station. Yaesu North Exit. Many regional handicrafts displayed by prefecture on the 8th and 9th floors of Daimaru and in approximately 30 showrooms in the adjacent Kokusai Kanko Building, floors 2,3 & 4. Hours 10-5:30. Sat. 10-12:30. Kokusai Tel. 3215-1181. Closed Sun. Daimaru closed Wed. Tel. 3212-8011.

PERIODIC MARKETS

Vendors from all parts of Japan assemble on a regular basis on the grounds of certain shrines, providing a rich sellection and a wide range of prices. These schedules are subject to change.

TOKYO

Arai Yakushi Antique Fair, 80 dealers
Arai Yakushi Temple, First Sunday of each month
10 minute walk from Arai Yakushi Station (Seibu Line)

Boro-ichi Antique Market, 50 dealers
Boro-ichi Street, December 15-16 and January 15-16
5 minute walk from Setagaya Station
(Tokyu Setagaya Line)

Hanazono Shrine Antique Market, 80 dealers
Hanazono Shrine, Second and Third Sundays
5 minute walk from Shinjuku San-chome Station
(Subway Marunouchi Line)

Heiwajima Antique Market, 200 dealers
Heiwajima-Tokyo Ryutsu Center Bldg. at Ryutsu
Center Station on Tokyo Monorail Line from
JR. Hamamatsucho Station. Three consecutive days,
four times a year in a modern exhibition hall
(with restaurant facilities). For exact dates, call
3950-0871. It is the most important single market
in Japan.

Ikebukuro Antique Market, 30 dealers
Ikebukuro Sunshine Bldg., Third Saturdays
and Sundays
10 minute walk from JR Ikebukuro Station

Nogizaka Antique Market, 50 dealers
Nogi Shrine, Second Sunday of each month
Nogizaka Station (Subway Chiyoda Line)

Ramla Antique Market
Ramla Bldg., First Saturday of each month
3 minute walk from JR Iidabashi Station

Roppongi Antique Fair, 30 dealers
Roppongi Roi Bldg., Fourth Thursdays and Fridays
10 minute walk from Roppongi Station
(Subway Hibiya Line)

Shofuda-kai Antique Market
Tokyo Bijutsu Club, Early July and Early December
(two days each, call 3431-6060 for exact dates).
15 minute walk from Onarimon Station
(Subway Mita Line)

Togo No Mori Antique Market, 70-90 dealers
Togo Shrine, First and Fourth Sunday of each month
10 minute walk from JR Harajuku Station

Tokyo Antique Hall
2-9, Kanda Surugadai, Chiyoda-ku, Tokyo
5 minute walk from JR Ochanomizu Station

Tokyo Antique Market, 30 dealers
Hanae Mori Bldg., 3-6, Kita Aoyama, Minato-ku, Tokyo
3 minute walk from Omote-sando Station
(Subway Ginza Line)

TOKYO SUBURBS

Kawagoe Antique Market, 50 dealers
Narita-fudo Temple, The 28th of each month
15 minute walk from Hon-Kawagoe Station
(Seibu Line)

Saiunji Temple, The 14th of each month
10 minute walk from Kawagoe Station (Seibu Line)

Sagami Antique Market, 10 dealers
Atsugi Shrine, First Saturday of each month
5 minute walk from Honatsugi Station (Odakyu Line)

Shonan Antique Market, 20 dealers
Yugyoji Temple, First Sunday of each month
20 minute walk from JR Fujisawa Station

Takahata Fudo Market, 15 dealers
Takahata Fudo Temple, Third Sunday of each month
5 minute walk from Takahata Fudo Station (Keio Line)

Urawa Antique Market, 30 dealers
Sakuraso Street, Fourth Saturday of each month
3 minute walk from JR Urawa Station

NAGANO

Karuizawa Antique Market
Kyu-Karuizawa Public Hall, August 1-31,
15 minute walk from JR Karuizawa Station

NAGOYA AREA

Henshoin Antique Market, 15 dealers
Henshoin Temple, Every 21st on Lunar Calendar
5 minute walk from Chiryu Station (Meitetsu Line)

Osu Kannon Antique Market, 30 dealers
Osu Kannon Temple, The 18th and 28th of
each month
Near Osu Kannonmae Station (Subway Tsurumai Line)

KYOTO

Kobo Antique Market, 50 dealers
Toji Temple, First Sundays, The 21st of each month
5 minute walk from Toji Station (Kintetsu Line)

Tenjin Antique Market, 100 dealers
Kitano Tenmangu Shrine, The 25th of each month
30 minutes by bus from JR Kyoto Station

OSAKA

Daishi Antique Market, 200 dealers
Osaka Shitennoji Temple, The 21st of each month
5 minute walk from Shitennojimae Station
(Subway Tanimachi Line)

Hatsu Tatsu Mairi Market, 25 dealers
Sumiyoshi Taisha Shrine, first Dragon Day of
each month
5 minute walk from Toriimae Station
(Nankai Hankai Line)

Koshindo Antique Market, 30 dealers
Koshindo Temple, Every Sunday
5 minute walk from Shitennoji-mae Station
(Subway Tanimachi Line)

Ohatsu Tenjin Antique Market, 12 dealers
Ohatsu Tenjin Shrine, First Friday of each month
5 minute walk from Umeda Station (Hanshin Line)

Sankaku Koen Antique Market
Sankaku Park, Every Sunday
5 minute walk from Dobutsuen-mae Station
(Subway Midosuji Line)

KOBE

Kobe Antique Market, 30 dealers
Sumadera Temple, First Sunday of each month
5 min. walk from Sumadera Station
(Sanyo Dentetsu Line)

HIROSHIMA AREA

Cancan Bazar (Kurashiki City), 30 dealers
Ivy Square, Consecutive national holidays
in May and Oct.
15 minute walk from JR Kurashiki Station

Sumiyoshi Antique Market (Fukuyama City)
10 dealers
Sumiyoshi Square, Fourth Sunday of each month
15 minute walk from JR Fukuyama Station

This sampling of sources for things Japanese for the home and garden also includes museum gift shops, which are indicated by an asterisk.

ARIZONA

Orient East
6204 N. Scottsdale Road
(Lincoln Village Shops)
Scottsdale 85253
(602) 948-0489
Furnishings, artifacts

CALIFORNIA

Abacus
628 Santa Cruz Avenue
Menlo Park 94025
(415) 323-5893
Antiques and folkcraft

Asakichi
1730 Geary Boulevard
San Francisco 94115
(415) 921-2147
Furniture, porcelain,
Japanese accessories

***Asian Art Museum
of San Francisco**
Avery Brundage Collection
Golden Gate Park
San Francisco 94118-4598
(415) 668-8921

Roger Barber
114 Pine Street
San Anselmo 94960
(415) 457-6844
Antiques

Elaine Barchan Interiors
2261 Highland Oaks Drive
Arcadia 91006
(818) 355-8674/ Fax 818-355-9340
By appointment
Antique textiles and obi

Blue Horizons
205 Florida Street
San Francisco 94103
(415) 626-1602
Shoji manufacturer specializing
in Western interior application

**Len Brackett
East Wind (Higashi Kaze), Inc.**
21020 Shields Camp Road
Nevada City 95959
(916) 265-3744
Construction of custom-built Japanese
homes/rooms.

Robert Brian Co.
Galleria/Design Center
101 Henry Adams, Space 136
San Francisco 94103
(415) 621-2273
Wide selection of antiques,
tansu and folkcraft.
Principally wholesale.

Bunka-Do
340 East First Street
Los Angeles 90012
(213) 625-1122
Paper, hanging scrolls, painted screens,
folkcraft, ceramics

Chadine Interior Design
15910 Ravine Road
Los Gatos 95030
(408) 354-0606
Interior designer and landscaper
specializing in Japanese aesthetics

The Crane and Turtle
Showplace Square West
550 15th Street
San Francisco 94103
(415) 861-9883
Wide collection of fine & folk
art, antique and contemporary

Dandelion
2877 California Street
San Francisco 94117
(415) 563-3100
Garden lanterns, basins, iron wind bells,
river stones, woodblock prints, obi,
ikebana and *bonsai* accessories,
ceramics, glassware, iron teapots and
tea accessories

Design Shoji
1850 Industrial Way
Redwood City 94063
(415) 363-0898/ Fax 415- 363-0899
Sales reps in several states
Custom-made *shoji*

Elica's Paper
1801 Fourth Street
Berkeley 94710
(510) 845-9530
Washi—wide selection of Japanese
handmade paper

Dodi Fromson Antiques
P.O. Box 49808
Los Angeles 90049
(310) 451-1110/Fax 310- 395-5737
By appointment
Antiques, textiles, bronzes,
metalwork, lacquerware

Fumiki Fine Arts
2001 Union St.
San Francisco 94123
(415) 922-0573
Obi, porcelain, *tansu, netsuke*

The Gallery
27 Malaga Cove Plaza
Palos Verdes Estates 90274
(310) 375-2212
Antiques

Genji
501 York St.
San Francisco 94110
(415) 255-2215
&
1731 Buchanan Street
San Francisco 94115
(415) 931-1616
Wide selection of chests,
folk art and kimono

Gump's
250 Post Street
San Francisco 94108
(415) 982-1616
800-652-1662 dialing within CA
800-227-3135 from out of state
&
9560 Wilshire Boulevard
Beverly Hills 92000
(213) 278-3200
Wide collection of antiques,
furniture and art objects

House of Crispo
425 Cannery Row
Monterrey 93940
(408) 373-8467
Porcelain, *netsuke,*
Oriental art

Imari Inc.
40 Filbert Avenue
Sausalito 94965
(415) 332-0245
Specialists in screens and fine antiques

International Trading Co.
950 E. 11th Street
Los Angeles 90012
(213) 629-5554
Noren, yukata

Japan Gallery
2624 Wilshire Boulevard
Santa Monica 90403
(213) 453-6406
Netsuke, tansu, baskets, kimono

The Japan Trading Co.
370 Barneveld Avenue
San Francisco 94124
(415) 282-3818 / Fax 415-282-2644
Shoji, tatami, fusuma

Japonesque
824 Montgomery Street
San Francisco 94133
(415) 391-8860
Wide selection of antique and
contemporary home furnishings

Kasuri Dye-Works
1959 Shattuck Avenue
Berkeley 94704
(415) 841-4509
Kasuri, silk, *yukata* fabric by
the yard, wooden folkcrafts.
Mail order video available

Kuromatsu
722 Bay Street
San Francisco 94109
(415) 474-4027
Antiques, folkcraft

Larchmont Japanese Antiques
115 N. Larchmont Boulevard
Los Angeles 90004
(213) 467-0430
Antiques

*Los Angeles County Museum of Art
Japanese Pavilion
5905 Wilshire Boulevard
Los Angeles 90036
Shops: (213) 857-6146,857- 6520
Books, art objects, paper products

Marukai Corp.
15725 S. Vermont Avenue
Gardena 90247
(213) 538-4025
Kimono

Marukyo U.S.A.
New Otani Hotel Arcade
110 S. Los Angeles Street
Los Angeles 90012
(213) 628-4369
Kimono, obi, fabrics

Marumasu
336 East Second Street
Los Angeles 90012
(213) 628-5198
Kimono

McMullen's Japanese Antiques
146 N. Robertson Boulevard
Los Angeles 90048
(310) 652-9492 / Fax 310- 652-2877
Tansu, folk art, lacquerware,
kimono, porcelain, ceramics,
obi, screens, *netsuke*

*The Metropolitan Museum of Art Shop
Century City Shop Center
10250 Santa Monica Blvd.,#102A
Los Angeles 90067
(310) 552-0905
&
South Coast Plaza
3333 Bristol Street
Costa Mesa 92626
(714) 435-9160
Changing collection of reproductions

Mikado (J.C. Trading, Inc.)
1737 Post Street
San Francisco 94115
(415) 922-9450
Kimono, *futon*, interior decorations

***Mingei International Museum
of World Folk Art**
4405 La Jolla Village Drive, Bldg. 1-7
San Diego 92122
(619) 453-5300

Nakura Inc.
252 Michelle Court
S. San Francisco 94080
(415) 588-6115 / Fax 415-588-6560
Tansu, antiques

Nichi Bei Bussan
1715 Buchanan Mall
San Francisco 94115
(415) 346-2117
&
140 Jackson Street
San Jose 95112
(408) 294-8048
Kimono, folk art, *noren*,
yukata by the yard

Shige Nishiguchi
Japan Center #204
1730 Geary Boulevard
San Francisco 94115
(415) 346-5567
Vintage kimono, antiques

Oriental Arts
1206 Orange Avenue
Coronado 92118
(619) 435-5451
Lacquerware, porcelain

Oriental Corner
280 Main Street
Los Altos 94022
(415) 941-3207
Antiques, *netsuke*, lacquerware,
porcelain

Oriental Porcelain Gallery
2702 Hyde Street
San Francisco 94109
(415) 776-5969
19th century porcelain

Oriental Treasure Box
Olde Cracker Factory
Antique Shopping Center
448 W. Market Street
San Diego 92101
(619) 233-3831
Tansu, kimono, obi, lacquerware, folk
art, porcelain, textiles, *hibachi*, dolls

Orientations
34 Maiden Lane
San Francisco 94108
(415) 981-397
Porcelain, baskets, *tansu*, screens

*Pacific Asia Museum
46 N. Los Robles Avenue
Pasadena 91101
(818) 449-2742

*Phoebe Hearst Museum of Anthropology
University of California
Campus at Berkeley, Kroeber Hall
(510) 643-7648, 642-3681

Sakura Horikiri USA, Inc.
19800 Hawthorne Blvd.
Suite 218
Torrance 90503
(310) 214-5055
Washi paper and *washi* craft kits
(pictures, jewelry, etc.)

*San Francisco Art Institute
800 Chestnut
San Francisco 94131
(415) 749-4555
Japanese papers

Shibui Japanese Antiques
991 East Green Street
Pasadena 91106
(818) 578-0908
Wide selection of antiques and folkcraft

Soko Hardware
1698 Post Street
San Francisco 94115
(415) 931-5510
Kites (upstairs), porcelain,
chopstick rests (downstairs)

Soko Hardware
1698 Post Street
San Francisco 94115
(415) 931-5510
Kites (upstairs), porcelain,
chopstick rests (downstairs)

Soko Interiors
1672 Post Street
San Francisco 94115
(415) 922-4155
Folkcraft, furniture,
lacquerware, porcelain

Takahashi Oriental Decor
235 15th Street
San Francisco 94103
(415) 552-5511
Wide selection of antiques and home
furnishings plus wood and bamboo
interior construction material, rope and
dry hedge landscape materials, garden
gates, *Jizo*, roof tiles

Takahashi Trading Corp.
200 Rhode Island St.
San Francisco 94103
(415) 431-8300
Screens, *shoji*, doors, *ranma*,
scrolls, paintings, classic calligraphy to
order, traditional paintings to order,
wooden carvings to order

Tampopo
410 Townsend St., Space 400
San Francisco 94107
(415) 979-0456
Traditional and contemporary arts and
crafts including cherrybark objects,
garden lanterns, woodblock prints,
ceramics, glassware, ironware,
ikebana/bonsai accessories. Wholesale
only. (Catalogue available to trade.)

Tansu Collections
Greta Vriend Weaver
Box 1396
Menlo Park 94025
(415) 323-6272
By appointment
Haori, tansu, textiles, *mingei*, lamps,
customized furniture

Townhouse Living
1825 Post Street
San Francisco 94115
(415) 568-1417
Kimono, obi, folkcraft, furniture

Warren Imports
Far East Fine Arts
1910 South Coast Highway
Laguna Beach 92651
(714) 494-6505/Fax 714-494-1067
&
73-199 El Paseo Avenue
Palm Desert 92660
(619) 340-9410 (619) 773-3023
Very large selection including *tansu,*
Imari, Satsuma, screens,obi, bronzes,
netsuke and garden lanterns

The Zentner Collection
5757 Landregan Street
Emeryville 94608
(510) 653-5181
Very large selection of
antiques, especially *tansu*
and *mingei*

COLORADO

Cherry Tree
P.O. Box 17815
Boulder 80308
Tel. and Fax (303) 442-4814
Handcrafted furnishings, *andon*, lamps,
shoji, and home accessories. Wholesale,
retail mail order, custom furnishings.
Catalog available.

CONNECTICUT

**Graynook Antiques and
Interiors**
72 Park Avenue
Bridgeport 06604
(203) 334-3621
By appointment
Wedding kimono, Imari

The Kura
310 Rockrimmon Road
Stamford 06903
(203) 329-1778
By appointment
Hibachi, tansu, lamps, obi,
baskets, screens

*The Metropolitan Museum of Art Shop
131 Westfarms Mall
Farmington 06032
(203) 561-5336
&
Stamford Town Center
100 Grey Rocks Place
Stamford 06901
(203) 978-0554
Changing collection of reproductions

Midori
7 Campbell Drive
Stamford 06903
(203) 322-9639
By appointment
Wide variety of antiques & folkcraft
including dolls, Imari, *tansu*

Stephen Morrell
57 Cedar Lake Road
Chester, CT 06412
(203) 526-1558
Landscape designer and lecturer
specializing in Japanese - style gardens

Silk Road Gallery
131 Post Road East
Westport 06880
(203) 221-9099
Hibachi, ranma, lacquerware,
ceramics,*tansu*, baskets, kimono, obi

Tradewinds
1749 House
Goshen 06756
(203) 491-2141
Antiques and artifacts

Vallin Galleries
516 Danbury Road (Rte. 7)
Wilton 06897
(203) 762-7441
Fine porcelain, *tansu, hibachi,*
stone lanterns, art

DELAWARE

A Touch of the Orient
Garrett Snuff Mills
Yorklyn 19736
(302) 239-4636/Fax 302- 234-2257
Tansu, antique furniture, dolls, kimono, obi

DISTRICT OF COLUMBIA

Arise Gallery
6295 Willow St., N.W.
Washington, D.C. 20012
(202) 291-0770
Kimono, obi,*tansu, hibachi*, screens,
ranma, dolls, baskets, porcelain, prints

Asian Art Center
2709 Woodley Pl., N.W.
Washington, D.C. 20008
(202) 234-3333
Porcelain, lacquerware, screens

*Freer Gallery of Art
Smithsonian Institution
Jefferson Dr. at 12th St., S.W.
Washington, D.C. 20560
(202) 357-1300 museum
(202) 357-1429 museum shop

Ginza "Things Japanese"
1721 Connecticut Ave., N.W.
Washington, D.C. 20009
(202) 331-7991
Folk art and crafts, pottery, kimono,
futon, shoji, stone lanterns, basins, books,
stationery, *ikebana/bonsai*, art supplies

*The Textile Museum
2320 S Street, N.W.
Washington, D.C. 20008
(202) 667-0441

FLORIDA

Carol Croll
Asian Accents
4238 45th St. S.
St. Petersburg 33711
Washi eggs, kimono, *washi* jewelry

Galleries
234 Worth Avenue
Palm Beach 33480
(407) 655-6114
Fine art

*Morikami Museum and
Japanese Gardens
4000 Morikami Park Road
Delray Beach 33446
(407) 495-0233
Gardens open daily. Museum and
shop closed Mondays

Vilda B. de Porro
311 & 209 Worth Avenue
Palm Beach 33480
(407) 655-3147
Hibachi

GEORGIA

J.H. Elliott Appraisal and
Antique Company
537 Peachtree Street, N.E.
Atlanta 30308
(404) 872-8233
Antiques

The Metropolitsan Museum of Art Shop
Lenox Square
3393 Peachtree Road NE
Atlanta 30326
(404) 264-1424
Changing collection of reproductions

Sahara Japanese Architectural
Woodworks, Inc.
1716 Defoor Place N.W.
Atlanta 30318
(404) 355-1976
Home construction, *shoji* screens,
teahouses, wood craft

HAWAII

Bushido
936 Maunakea Street
Honolulu 96817
(808) 536-5693
Fax: (808) 521-1994
Ceramics, kimono, obi, swords

Garakuta-do
444 Hobron Lane PH-1
Honolulu 96815
(808) 955-2099 /Fax 808-955-3450
Tansu, Imari, *mingei*, textiles

*Honolulu Academy of Arts
900 South Beretania Street
Honolulu 96814
(808) 532-8703/ Fax 808-532-8787

Amaury Saint-Gilles
P.O. Box E
Papa'aloa, Hawaii 96780
Tel. and Fax (808) 962-6884
By appointment only
Contemporary fine art, graphics and
ceramics.

Upstairs Gallery/Kohala Kollection
Kawaihoe Shopping Center
P.O. Box 44554
Kamuela, Hawaii 96743
(808) 882-1304 Fax (808) 882-1407
Wide selection of antiques and
oriental artwork

ILLINOIS

Aiko's Art Materials
3347 N-Clark St.
Chicago 60657
(312) 404-5600
Washi, contemporary prints

Saito Oriental Antiques, Inc.
Suite 428
645 North Michigan Avenue
Chicago 60611
(312) 642-4366
By appointment
Porcelain, bronzes, sculpture,
lacquerware, woodblock prints,
antique paintings

J. Toguri Mercantile Co.
851 West Belmont Avenue
Chicago 60657
(312) 929-3500
Home furnishings, lacquerware,
kimono

KENTUCKY

Boones Antiques
4996 Old Versailles Road
Lexington 40504
(606) 254-5335
Porcelain, furniture
8:30-5:30 Mon-Sat

*Headley-Whitney Museum
4435 Old Franklin Pike
Lexington 40510
(606) 255-6653
Porcelain, Decorative art

Wakefield-Scearce
525 Washington Street
Shelbyville 40065
(502) 633-4382
Masks, porcelain

LOUISIANA

New Orleans Museum of Art
City Park
New Orleans 70100
(504) 488-2631
Large collection of Asian art

Oriental Art and Antiques of
Diane Genre
233 Royal Street
New Orleans 70130
(504) 525-7270 /Fax 504-525-7281
Antiques, screens, furniture,
prints, textiles and lacquerware

MAINE

Ross Levett Antiques
Tenants Harbor 04843
(207) 372-8407
Antiques

Sign of the Owl
Coastal Route 1
Northport
Mailing address: P.O. Box 85 RR2
Lincolnville 04849
(207) 338-4669
Changing collection including *netsuke*,
inros, vases, porcelain,Kutani,Satsuma

MARYLAND

Knight-Flight
P.O. Box 1971
Frederick 21702-0971
(301) 695-2890
Porcelain, pottery, furniture, textiles,
silver, bronzes, woodblock prints, interior
decoration and appraisal services

Shogun Gallery
P.O. Box 5300
Gaithersburg 20882
(800) 926-4255/ Fax 301-948-0899
Woodblock prints, sword guards, dolls,
netsuke

MASSACHUSETTS

Alberts-Langdon, Inc.
126 Charles Street
Boston 02114
(617) 523-5954
Furniture, paintings, porcelain

Bernheimer's Antique Arts
52-C Brattle Street
Cambridge 02138
(617) 547-1117
Ceramics, prints, paintings,
netsuke, mingei

*Children's Museum
300 Congress Street
Boston 02210
(617) 426-6500

Eastern Accent
237 Newbury Street
Boston 02116
(617) 266-9707
Contemporary, handcrafted
designs for dining and the home.

Robert C. Eldred Co., Inc.
1483 Route 6A
East Dennis 02641
(508) 385-3116
Wide selection of antiques,
arts and accessories

*Isabella Stewart Gardner Museum
280 The Fenway
Boston 02115
(617) 566-1401

Kiku Sui Gallery
101 Charles Street
Boston 02114
(617) 227-4288
Antique and modern prints

Samuel L. Lowe, Jr. Antiques
80 Charles Street
Boston 02114
(617) 742-0845
Antiques, porcelain, prints

*Museum of Fine Arts, Boston
465 Huntington Avenue
Boston 02115
(617) 267-9300

***George Walter Vincent
Smith Art Museum**
222 State Street
Springfield 01103
(413) 733-4214

*Peabody Museum of Salem
161 Essex
Salem 01970
(617) 745-9500
Folkcraft

Sanpho America
189 State Street
Boston 02109
(617) 720-5370
Folkcraft, kimono, furniture

Vilunya Folk Art
Vilunya Diskin
Charles Square 5 Bennett Street
Cambridge 02138
(617) 661-5753
Folkcraft, kimono, *hanten*, obi, *haori*,
lacquered boxes

Zen Associates, Inc.
70 Love Lane
Concord 01742
(508) 369-6654/ Fax 508-369-3257
Landscape architecture
(interior, exterior), estate design

MICHIGAN

D and J Bittker Gallery Ltd.
536 N. Woodward
Birmingham 48011
(313) 258-1670
Antiques

Dulany's Gallery
4000 Quarton Road
Bloomfield Hills 48013
(313) 645-2233 or 645-7475
Antiques

MINNESOTA

Asian Fine Arts
850 Baker Bldg.
Minneapolis 55402
(612) 333-4740
Antique and contemporary
artwork, specializing in woodblock prints

Sharen Chappell
P.O. Box 9091
North St. Paul 55109
(612) 777-8910
Netsuke, lacquerware

MISSISSIPPI

East West Antiques
400 Cherokee Drive
McComb 39648
(601) 684-4638/ Fax 601-684-8565
Large selection of antique silk obi

MISSOURI

Asiatica Ltd.
4824 Rainbow Blvd.
Westwood, Kansas 66205
(913) 831-1110
Furniture, textiles, kimono,
obi, *mingei*

Brookside Antiques
6219 Oak Street
Kansas City 64113
(816) 444-4774
Furniture, woodblock prints,
porcelain, cloisonné

*Nelson-Atkins Museum of Art
4525 Oak Street
Kansas City 64111
(816) 561-4000

NEW JERSEY

Ivory Bird
555 Bloomfield Avenue
Montclair 07000
(201) 744-5225
Imari, prints, embroidery

The Metropolitan Museum of Art Shop
Mall at Short Hills
Short Hills 07078
(201) 376-4466
Changing collection of reproductions

Tsuru Gallery
41 Valley Crest Road
Annandale 07401
(201) 772-6422
Woodblock prints, screens, paintings

NEW MEXICO

Five Eggs
Plaza Mercado 212 B
112 West San Francisco St.
Santa Fe 87501
(505) 986-3403
Antiques, traditional *futons*, kimono,
ceramics, *mingei, yukata, tatami*

Mary Hunt Kahlenberg
1571 Canyon Road
Santa Fe 87501
(505) 983-9780 by appointment
Textile arts

Little Shop
Water Street Plaza
138 West Water Street
Santa Fe 87501
(505) 984-1050
Fine art

NEW YORK

A/N/W Crestwood
315 Hudson Street
New York City 10013
(212) 989-2700
Toll Free:800-525-3196/Fax:212- 929-7532
Largest importer of Oriental
papers in U.S. Call for retail sources
in 50 states, Canada and abroad

Art Asia, Inc.
1088 Madison Avenue (81st St.)
New York City 10028
(212) 249-7250
Kimono, obi, lacquerware,
porcelain, baskets, furniture

Asia Society
725 Park Avenue
New York City 10021
(212) 288-6400
Keyaki stationery boxes, ironware
teapots, ceremonial teacups—
Shino ware

Azuma Gallery
50 Walker Street
New York City 10013
(212) 925-1381
Woodblock prints, ceramics,
sculpture, swords

Bonsai Designs
1862 Newbridge Road
North Bellmore 11710
(516) 785-5397
Nursery plus custom-designed
interiors and exteriors

*Brooklyn Museum
200 Eastern Parkway
Brooklyn 11238
(718) 638-5000

Daikichi
Madison Street
Sag Harbor 11963
(516) 725-1533
In Manhattan by appointment:
(212) 532-2192
Wide variety of furnishings
and textiles

Eastern Dreams
6 Greenridge Drive
Chappaqua 10514
(914) 666-8910
By appointment only
Porcelain, *yukata*, lacquerware,
paper and wood crafts, *ikebana*
planters, contemporary screens

Edo Antiques Ltd.
67 East 11th Street
New York City 11011
(212) 254-2508
Furniture, porcelain, art

David H. Engel
Landgarden
215 Park Avenue South
New York 10003
(212) 228-9500
Landscape architects

Felissimo
10 West 56th Street
New York City 10019
(212) 247-5656
Innovative designs by environmentally
aware artisans—gifts, tableware and
handcrafted home furnishings—
displayed in a 100-year-old brownstone

Flying Cranes Antiques
Manhattan Art & Antique Center
1050 Second Avenue (56th St.)
New York City 10022
(212) 223-4600
Antiques—Imari, bronzes, samurai swords
and armor, silver, cloisonné,
money chests

Gallery Zero
236 E. 49th Street
New York City 10017
(212) 397-2800
Fine Japanaese ceramics
2:00-6:00 Mon-Sat

Gordon Foster Antiques
1322 Third Avenue (75th St.)
New York City 10021
(212) 744-4922
Mingei, baskets, *tansu*, ceramics,
porcelain

Charles R. Gracie & Sons, Inc.
979 Third Avenue
New York City 10022
(212) 753-5350
Tansu, hibachi, screens

Grillion Corporation
189-193 First Street
Brooklyn 11215
(718) 875-8545
Shoji

Hayama
19 Main Street
Southampton 11968
(516) 283-4182
Porcelain, *tansu*, screens, *mingei*, lacquer

Inouye Japanese Gardens, Inc.
75 North Woodhull Rd.
Huntington 11743
(516) 421-0990
Landscaping, interior/exterior design
and construction, teahouses,
rock gardens

*Japan Society
333 East 47th Street
New York City 10017
(212) 832-1155

Japanese Screen
23-37 91st Street
East Elmhurst 11369
(718) 803-2267
Shoji, tatami, fusuma, lamps

Kate's Paperie
8 West 13th Street
New York City 10011
(212) 633-0570
&
561 Broadway
New York City 10012
(212) 941-9816
Wide selection of *washi*

Kimono House
120 Thompson St.
New York City 10012
(212) 966-5936
Antique kimono and small items

Koto
71 West Houston Street
New York City 10012
(212) 533-8601
Kimono, lacquerware, screens,
contemporary ceramics, crafts

Leighton R. Longhi
P.O. Box 6704
New York City 10128
Fax: (212) 996-0721
Museum quality fine art

Lord & Taylor
424 Fifth Avenue
New York City 10018
(212) 391-3344
Tansu (8th floor),
antique Imari (9th floor)

*Metropolitan Museum of Art
1000 Fifth Avenue
New York City 10028
(212) 879-5500
Gift shop: *netsuke*, lacquerware,
ceramics, posters
&
Rockefeller Plaza
15 W. 49th Street
New York City 10020
(212) 332-1360
&
New York Public Library
455 Fifth Avenue
New York City 10016
(212) 679-677
&
The Americana Shopping Center
2106 Northern Blvd.
Manhasset 11030
(516) 627-7474
Changing collection of reproductions

Miya Shoji & Interiors, Inc.
109 West 17th Street
New York City 10011
(212) 243-6774
Japanese rooms, *shoji, fusuma,* light
fixtures, stone lanterns

Naga Antiques Ltd.
145 East 61st Street
New York City 10021
(212) 593-2788
Fax (212) 308-2451
Fine collection of antique Japanese
screens, lacquerware, sculpture,
ceramics and objets d'art displayed
in a garden brownstone.

Orientations Gallery
802 Madison Avenue
New York City 10021
(212) 371-9006
19th century decorative art,
cloisonné, Satsuma, metalwork, inlaid
bronzes, ivory, wood carvings, silver,
netsuke, art lacquer, *inro, ojime*

Pillow Perfections
12 Stuyvesant Street
New York City 10003
(212) 528-5183
Tatami

Ronin Gallery
605 Madison Avenue
New York City 10022
(212) 688-0188
Woodblock prints (17th through
20th century), *netsuke*, pottery,
sword guards

Sugimoto
120 East 64th Street
New York City 10021
(212) 751-0650
By appointment only
Museum quality antique art and
sculpture, antique and contemporary
ceramics, archeological pieces

Takashimaya
693 Fifth Avenue
New York City 10022
(212) 350-0100/Fax 212-350-0542
Screens, *tansu*, baskets, lacquerware,
porcelain

Talas
213 W. 35th Street
New York City 10001
(212) 736-7744 / Fax 212- 465-8722
Closed from 11:30–1:00 Mon. thru Fri.
Handmade Japanese paper

Tansuya Corporation
159 Mercer Street
New York City 10001
(212) 966-1782
Furniture, screens, lacquerware

Tenjin Gallery
17 Brook Street
Staten Island 10301
(718) 273-0566
Ceramics, textiles, prints, *tansu, mingei*

Terracotta
The John Rogers Collection
2 Main Street
Southampton 11968
(516) 283-7209/ Fax 516-283-5952
Lacquerware, gifts, home furnishings

Things Japanese
127 E. 60th Street
New York City 10022
(212) 249-3591/ Fax 212-465-8722
Woodblock prints,*mingei*, kimono, obi,
baskets, Imari, furniture, *netsuke*, dolls

Tokyo Arts Salon
Manhattan Art & Antique Center
1050 Second Avenue (56th St.)
New York City 10022
(212) 888-7195
Kimono, antique Imari

Joanne Wise
The Wise Collection
4 Morningside Circle
Bronxville 10708
(914) 961-9325/ Fax 914-793-7220
Contemporary paintings, prints,
pottery and sculpture

Yuzen Ltd.
318 East 6th Street
New York City 10003
(212) 473-3405
Kimono, wedding kimono, *yukata*,
antique and contemporary

Zen Oriental Bookstore
521 Fifth Avenue
New York City 10017
(212) 697-0840
Washi, ceramics, dolls

OHIO

Mary Baskett Gallery
1002 St. Gregory Street
Cincinnati 45202
(513) 421-0460
Ceramics, Oriental art

Ginko Tree
Dillonvale Shopping Center
4389 East Galbraith Road
Deerpark, Cincinnati
(513) 984-0553
Ceramics, porcelain

*Cleveland Museum of Art
1150 East Boulevard
Cleveland 44106
(216) 421-0931/ Fax 216-421-0424
Books, posters, notecards, postcards

The Metropolitan Museum of Art Shop
352 Columbus City Center Drive
Columbus 43215
(614) 221-7886
Changing collection of reproductions

Mitzie Verne Collection
2207 Murray Hill Road
Cleveland 44106
(216) 231-8866
Mail to: 3326 Lansmere Road
Shaker Heights 44122
Contemporary & antique prints,
hand stencil dyed prints, screens,
scrolls, contemporary ceramics

OREGON

Shibumi Trading Ltd.
P.O. Box 1-F
Eugene 97440
Outside of Oregon:
1-800-843-2565
In Oregon: (503) 744-1832
Antique kimono, obi, books, stone
lanterns, basins, wide selection of
folkcraft. Mail order catalog available.

Shogun's Gallery
206 Northwest 23rd Avenue
Portland 97210
(503) 224-0328
Tansu, mingei, textiles, porcelain

PENNSYLVANIA

Pearl of the East
Willow Grove Park
Springfield Mall
1615 Walnut Street
Philadelphia 19100
(215) 563-1563
Furnishings, porcelain,
futon bedding

Three Cranes Gallery
82 South Main St.
New Hope 18938
(215) 862-5626
Tansu, porcelain, textiles, prints,
shoji, tatami, scrolls, screens,
contemporary art

RHODE ISLAND

Nortons' Oriental Gallery
415 Thames Street
Newport 02840
(401) 849-4468
Antiques

Oriental Arts Ltd.
Brickmarket Place
Newport 02840
(401) 846-0655
Antiques, reproductions, accessories
and furniture

SOUTH CAROLINA

The Red Torii
197 King Street
Charleston 29401
(803) 723-0443
Porcelain, *netsuke*, bronzes, cloisonné

TEXAS

Asian Arts
1980 Post Oak Boulevard
Houston 77000
(713) 629-9797
Antiques and art

*Kimbell Art Museum
3333 Camp Bowie Blvd.
Fort Worth 76107
(817) 332-8451

East & Orient Company
2901 North Henderson
Dallas 75206
(214) 826-1191/ Fax 214-821-8632
Porcelain, lacquerware, screens

Janet Lashbrooke
Oriental Antiques
112 Sugarberry Circle
Houston 77024
(713) 953-9144
Tansu, mingei, baskets, teapots

Loyd-Paxton, Inc.
3636 Maple Avenue
Dallas 75219
(214) 521-1521
Textiles, lacquerware, screens,
porcelain, bronzes, cloisonné

The Metropolitan Museum Gift Shop
Houston Galleria
5015 Westheimer Suite 2440
Houston 77056
(713) 629-1515/ Fax 713-629-1525
Changing collection of reproductions

Translations
4811 Abbott
Dallas 75205
(214) 522-1115, 351-0285
By appointment
Home accessories, antique and
contemporary

WASHINGTON

Asia Gallery
1220 First Avenue
Seattle 98101
(206) 622-0516
Wide selection of antiques &
folkcraft, including textiles,
furniture, baskets, masks,
porcelain

The Crane Gallery, Inc.
1203 B Second Avenue
Seattle 98101
(206) 622-7185
Asian art

Honeychurch Antiques Ltd.
1008 James Street
Seattle 98104
(206) 622-1225
Furniture, ceramics, paintings,
woodblock prints, sculptures,
stone water basins, lanterns

Japanese Antiquities Gallery
200 East Boston Street
Seattle 98102
(206) 324-3322
Monday through Friday 9-4,
Saturday by appointment
Antique folk art, furniture, ceramics

Kagedo
520 First Avenue South
Seattle 98104
(206) 467-9077
Bronzes, lacquers, *tsuba, tansu* and furnishings, architectural carvings, garden
stones, silk kimono and other textiles

Marvel on Madison
69 Madison
Seattle 98104
(206) 624-4225
Folkcrafts, ceramics, *tansu,* lacquerware

Andy Shiga's One World Shop
4306 University Way NE
Seattle 98100
(206) 633-2400
Kimono

*Seattle Art Museum
14th E. & E. Prospect
Seattle 98100
(206) 625-8900
Textiles, art

Uwajimaya
6th Ave. S. and S. King St.
Seattle 98104
(206) 624-6248
&
N.E. 24th and Bel-Red Road
Bellevue 98007
(206) 747-9012
Washi, shoji lamps, kimono, *noren,*
ikebana vases

CANADA

TORONTO

Dolly Beil Ltd.
986 Eglinton Avenue, W.
Toronto, Ontario M6C 2C5
(416) 781-2334
Kutani & Satsuma porcelain

Gallery Shioda
98 Avenue Road
Toronto, Ontario M5R 2H3
(416) 961-2066
Wide selection of antiques,
including kimono, *hibachi* and *tansu*

Japanese Paper Place
887 Queen Street, W.
Toronto, Ontario M6J 1G5
(416) 369-0089
Washi, including *shoji,* stencilled
paper and paper for origami,
books on paper art

Okame Japanese Antiques
David Pepper
709 Devonshire Road
Windsor, Ontario N8Y 2L9
(519) 253-0336
By appointment
Ceramics, antique textiles, baskets,
scrolls, dolls, metalwork, woodblock
prints, folk art & lacquer. Appraisals and
restoration, design consultant.

Ozawa Canada Inc.
135 E. Beaver Creek Rd., Unit 3
Richmond Hill, Ontario L4B 1E2
(412) 229-6343/ Fax 416- 731-0778
Tea chests, fine chinaware, kitchen
equipment, housewares, *shoji* screens,
tatami, garden lanterns

VANCOUVER

Japanese Accents Kiku
1532 Marine Drive
West Vancouver, B.C. V7V 1H8
(604) 925-2584
Tansu, chabako, mingei, textiles
and ceramics

Dorian Rae Collection
3151 Granville Street
Vancouver, B.C. V6H 3K1
(604) 732-6100
&
2033 West 4th Avenue
Vancouver B.C.
(604) 732-6100
Paintings, screens, dolls, ceramics,
hibachi

Frankie Robinson
Oriental Gallery
3055 Granville Street
Vancouver, B.C. V6H 3J9
(604) 734-6568
Tansu, mingei, Satsuma,
hibachi, screens

A C K N O W L E D G E M E N T S

Profound thanks to the dedicated and talented home-owners who so graciously opened their doors to us... to Hisao Hanafusa and Chadine Flood Gong, who provided key introductions... and to Toshiaki Sakuma, whose patience rivals his photographic talents. Thanks, Richard Reitzes, for convincing Jean to replace her reliable drawing board with a magical computer. And to Joseph Palys for leading her through its disconcerting mysteries... We are grateful to Ed Woodyard, master of the smooth segue... to Roland Reisley and Len Brackett for their technical advice... and finally to Shunichi "Sean" Kamiya, visionary editor whom we are proud to call friend.